A Practitioner's Guide to Factor Models

The Research Foundation of
The Institute of Chartered Financial Analysts

Research Foundation Publications

Active Currency Management
by Murali Ramaswami

*Canadian Stocks, Bonds, Bills, and
Inflation: 1950–1987*
by James E. Hatch and Robert E. White

*Closed-Form Duration Measures and
Strategy Applications*
by Nelson J. Lacey and Sanjay K. Nawalkha

*Corporate Bond Rating Drift: An
Examination of Credit Quality Rating
Changes over Time*
by Edward I. Altman and Duen Li Kao

*Default Risk, Mortality Rates, and the
Performance of Corporate Bonds*
by Edward I. Altman

Durations of Nondefault-Free Securities
by Gerald O. Bierwag and George G.
Kaufman

Earnings Forecasts and Share Price Reversals
by Werner F.M. De Bondt

*The Effect of Illiquidity on Bond Price Data:
Some Symptoms and Remedies*
by Oded Sarig and Arthur Warga

Equity Trading Costs
by Hans R. Stoll

*Ethics, Fairness, Efficiency, and Financial
Markets*
by Hersh Shefrin and Meir Statman

Ethics in the Investment Profession: A Survey
by E. Theodore Veit, CFA, and Michael R.
Murphy, CFA

*The Founders of Modern Finance: Their
Prize-Winning Concepts and 1990 Nobel
Lectures*

Franchise Value and the Price/Earnings Ratio
by Martin L. Leibowitz and Stanley Kogelman

*Global Asset Management and Performance
Attribution*
by Denis S. Karnosky, Ph.D., and Brian D.
Singer, CFA

*Initial Public Offerings: The Role of Venture
Capitalists*
by Joseph T. Lim and Anthony Saunders

The Modern Role of Bond Covenants
by Ilene B. Malitz

*A New Method for Valuing Treasury Bond
Futures Options*
by Ehud I. Ronn and Robert R. Bliss, Jr.

A New Perspective on Asset Allocation
by Martin L. Leibowitz

Options and Futures: A Tutorial
by Roger G. Clarke

*The Poison Pill Anti-Takeover Defense: The
Price of Strategic Deterrence*
by Robert F. Bruner

*Predictable Time-Varying Components of
International Asset Returns*
by Bruno Solnik

Program Trading and Systematic Risk
by A.J. Senchack, Jr., and John D. Martin

*The Role of Risk Tolerance in the Asset
Allocation Process: A New Perspective*
by W.V. Harlow III, CFA, and Keith C.
Brown, CFA

Selecting Superior Securities
by Marc R. Reinganum

Stock Market Structure, Volatility, and Volume
by Hans R. Stoll and Robert E. Whaley

*Stocks, Bonds, Bills, and Inflation:
Historical Returns (1926–1987)*
by Roger G. Ibbotson and Rex A.
Sinquefield
(Published with Irwin Professional
Publishing)

A Practitioner's Guide to
Factor Models

ISBN 0-943205-24-7

Printed in the United States of America

March 1994

Mission

The mission of the Research Foundation is to identify, fund, and publish research material that:
- expands the body of relevant and useful knowledge available to practitioners;
- assists practitioners in understanding and applying this knowledge; and
- enhances the investment management community's effectiveness in serving clients.

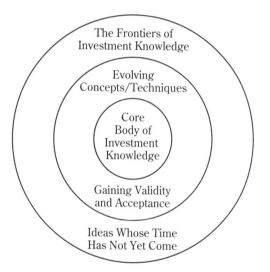

The Research Foundation of
The Institute of Chartered Financial Analysts
P. O. Box 3668
Charlottesville, Virginia 22903
U.S.A.
Telephone: 804/977-6600
Fax: 804/977-1103

Table of Contents

Foreword

Ever since the seminal work of Harry M. Markowitz (1952), the identification and measurement of investment risk have been hotly debated. Markowitz constructed a mean–variance model to demonstrate how to quantify both the risk and return of an asset or a portfolio of assets. The Markowitz model reveals that, in an efficient marketplace, higher returns can be accomplished only by accepting greater risks. Consequently, one of the most widely accepted financial principles is the tradeoff between risk and return.

Although the concept of investment risk is universally recognized, the appropriate measure of risk remains controversial. Financial researchers generally agree that specific (nonsystematic) risks, such as those pertaining only to individual companies, tend to cancel out in well-diversified portfolios. Because systematic risk is nondiversifiable, however, it cannot be eliminated. The first theory to measure systematic risk was the capital asset pricing model (CAPM) for which William F. Sharpe (1964) shared the 1990 Nobel Memorial Prize in Economic Sciences. The CAPM postulates that a single type of risk, known as market risk, affects expected security returns. Only by exposing a well-diversified portfolio to higher market risk can an investor expect to achieve a higher rate of return.

Under the CAPM, market risk is defined as the variability of an asset's rate of return relative to that of the overall market as measured by some market index such as the S&P 500. Beta, the coefficient of the independent variable (the market's rate of return) in an ordinary least squares regression equation to explain the dependent variable (a security's rate of return), measures a security's relative amount of systematic (market) risk. A beta equal to 1.0 indicates risk equivalent to that of the overall market, whereas a beta less than 1.0 denotes lower-than-market risk and a beta exceeding 1.0 indicates greater-than-market risk.

The arbitrage pricing theory (APT), first presented by Stephen A. Ross (1976), was the next major asset pricing model to appear. Also focusing on systematic risk, the APT recognizes that several different broad risk sources may combine to influence security returns. The intuitive appeal of the APT results from its recognition that the interaction of several macroeconomic factors such as inflation, interest rates, and business activity affects rates of return. The statistical process of factor analysis is employed to quantify the broad risk factors and to estimate individual securities' degree of exposure to these factors. A security effectively has a sensitivity to each systematic risk factor. A series of beta coefficients are estimated to measure the sensitivity to the respective factor risks for a particular security. Unlike the CAPM, however, the individual factors, although precisely quantified, are not specifically associated with readily identifiable variables. Although considerable discussion continues about the number and the identification of these broad factors, the APT nevertheless provides investment managers with a valuable risk-management tool.

Factor models, the focus of this monograph, have existed for many years. Even before the introduction of the popular CAPM and APT, Markowitz (1959) proposed the use of a single-factor model to explain security returns. Sometimes referred to as index models, factor models often rely on the use of factor analysis to identify factors that influence security returns.

A good portfolio manager, whether explicitly or implicitly, evaluates the impact of a series of broad factors on the performances of various securities. In this sense, a reliable factor model provides a valuable tool to assist portfolio managers with the identification of pervasive factors that affect large members of securities. According to a factor model, the return-generating process for a security is driven by the presence of the various common factors and the security's unique sensitivities to each factor (factor loadings). The common factors may be readily identifiable fundamental factors such as price–earnings ratio, size, yield, and growth. Factor models can be used to decompose portfolio risk according to common factor exposure and to evaluate how much of a portfolio's return was attributable to each common factor exposure. Consequently, factor models offer a useful extension of the CAPM and the APT because they advance our understanding about how key factors influence portfolio risk and return.

The CAPM is clear about the source of risk (the market) but suffers because no practical measure of the market exists. The APT causes difficulties because it does not identify the number of important factors or define them. Financial researchers and investment managers undoubtedly agree that only a few important factors explain an overwhelming degree of investment risk and return. Therefore, the appeal of factor models that define these factors becomes apparent.

Sharpe (1984) effectively summarizes why investment professionals should pay heed to factor models:

> While the relative importance of various actors changes over time, as do the preferences of investors, we need not completely abandon a valuable framework within which we can approach investment decisions methodically. We have developed a useful set of tools and should certainly continue to develop them. Meanwhile, we can use the tools we have, as long as we use them intelligently, cautiously, and humbly.

In this monograph, prominent academic and professional researchers of factor models unite to present a practitioner's guide to factor models. In the first article, Edwin Burmeister (Duke University), Richard Roll (University of California, Los Angeles), and Stephen Ross (Yale University) offer "A Practitioner's Guide to Arbitrage Pricing Theory." The authors not only explain the basics and the equations of APT but also discuss the macroeconomic forces that are the underlying sources of risk and how these factors combine to influence rates of return. Importantly, they present several ways for investment professionals to use APT effectively.

In the second article, Edwin J. Elton and Martin J. Gruber, both of New York University, present "Multi-Index Models Using Simultaneous Estimation of All Parameters." Beginning with an explanation of a single-factor model, the authors next discuss multi-index models. They point out that the familiar single-factor model provides a useful framework within which to compare multi-index models. Their article examines methodology for simultaneously estimating the indexes and sensitivities in a multi-index model. In addition, the authors carefully test factor models, thus providing guidance with respect to the reliability and usefulness of these models.

In the third article, Richard C. Grinold and Ronald N. Kahn, both of BARRA, address "Multiple-Factor Models for Portfolio Risk." They present a practical application of factor models to predict and control investment risk. Using a widely recognized multiple-factor risk model developed at BARRA, Grinold and Kahn emphasize the importance of identifying key fundamental factors that are relatively easy for investment professionals to use. They stress the use of factors that represent the recognized key investment attributes—volatility, momentum, size, liquidity, growth, value, earnings volatility, and financial leverage—and present specific measures of each. Thus, they advance the factor model literature by moving from quantitative, but unspecified, factors to readily identifiable fundamental characteristics.

As a result of the availability of substantial amounts of data and the increasing complexity of the investment decision-making process, the use of quantitative models now has heightened prominence in investment management. Factor models provide a useful extension of existing asset pricing models and allow managers to decompose portfolios into sensitivities to broad factors. This approach provides invaluable information about the attributes that influence portfolio returns, thus allowing managers to explain these returns.

Although the mathematics of factor models may be complex, the underlying concept is intuitively apparent. This series of articles explains factor models in ways that investment practitioners can understand and use. The Research Foundation of the Institute of Chartered Financial Analysts is pleased to sponsor "A Practitioner's Guide to Factor Models." It is our hope and belief that these articles will further the understanding and use of these valuable concepts.

John W. Peavy III, CFA

A Practitioner's Guide to Arbitrage Pricing Theory

Edwin Burmeister
Duke University

Richard Roll
University of California, Los Angeles

Stephen A. Ross
Yale University

A fundamental principle of finance is the trade-off between risk and return. Unless a portfolio manager possesses special information, one portfolio can be expected to outperform another only if it is riskier in some appropriate sense. The crucial question is: "What is the appropriate measure of risk?"

Many attributes might be related to an asset's risk, including market capitalization (size), dividend yield, growth, price–earnings ratio (P/E), and so on. Use of these traditional descriptors, however, presents at least three problems:

1. Most are based on accounting data, and such data are generated by rules that may differ significantly across firms.

2. Even if all firms used the same accounting rules, reporting dates differ, so constructing time-synchronized interfirm comparisons is difficult.

3. Most importantly, no rigorous theory tells us how traditional accounting variables should be related to an appropriate measure of risk for computing the risk–return trade-off. Even if historical empirical relationships can be uncovered, without the foundation of a rigorous theory, one must be concerned that any historical correlation might be spurious and subject to sudden and material change.

1

Currently, only two theories provide a rigorous foundation for computing the trade-off between risk and return: the capital asset pricing model (CAPM) and the arbitrage pricing theory (APT).

The CAPM, for which William F. Sharpe shared the 1990 Nobel Memorial Prize in Economic Sciences, predicts that only one type of nondiversifiable risk influences expected security returns, and that single type of risk is "market risk."[1] In 1976, a little more than a decade after the CAPM was proposed, Stephen A. Ross invented the APT. The APT is more general than the CAPM in accepting a variety of different risk sources. This accords with the intuition that, for example, interest rates, inflation, and business activity have important impacts on stock return volatility.

Although some theoretical formulations of the APT can be more intellectually demanding than the CAPM, the intuitively appealing basics behind the APT are easy to understand. Moreover, the APT provides a portfolio manager with a variety of new and easily implemented tools to control risks and to enhance portfolio performance.

In the remainder of this paper, we will explain APT basics and the equations of the APT. We will also discuss macroeconomic forces that are the underlying sources of risk. We will then illustrate some risk exposure profiles and the resulting APT-based risk–return trade-offs, and we will show how these fundamental risks contribute to the expected and unexpected components of realized return. Finally, we will discuss several uses of the APT that every practitioner could easily apply.

The APT Basics

The CAPM and the APT agree that, although many different firm-specific forces can influence the return on any individual stock, these idiosyncratic effects tend to cancel out in large and well-diversified portfolios. This cancellation is called the *principle of diversification*, and it has a long history in the field of insurance. An insurance company has no way of knowing whether any particular individual will become sick or will be involved in an accident, but the company is able to predict its losses accurately on a large pool of such risks.

---

[1] More precisely, if $r_m(t)$ is the return (in time period t) on a market index, such as the S&P 500, the CAPM measure of the riskiness for asset i with return $r_i(t)$ is equal to that asset's CAPM beta defined by $\beta_i = \text{cov}[r_i(t), r_m(t)]/\text{var}[r_m(t)]$.

The CAPM is equivalent to the statement that the market index is itself mean–variance efficient in the sense of providing maximum average return for a given level of volatility. The index used to implement the CAPM is implicitly assumed to be an effective proxy for the entire market of assets.

An insurance company is not entirely free of risk, however, simply because it insures a large number of individuals. For example, natural disasters or changes in health care can have major influences on insurance losses by simultaneously affecting many claimants. Similarly, large, well-diversified portfolios are not risk free, because common economic forces pervasively influence all stock returns and are not eliminated by diversification. In the APT, these common forces are called *systematic* or *pervasive risks*.

According to the CAPM, systematic risk depends only upon exposure to the overall market, usually proxied by a broad stock market index, such as the S&P 500. This exposure is measured by the CAPM *beta*, as defined in Footnote 1. Other things equal, a beta greater (less) than 1.0 indicates greater (less) risk relative to swings in the market index.[2]

The APT takes the view that systematic risk need not be measured in only one way. Although the APT is completely general and does not specify exactly what the systematic risks are, or even how many such risks exist, academic and commercial research suggests that several primary sources of risk consistently impact stock returns. These risks arise from unanticipated changes in investor confidence, interest rates, inflation, real business activity, and a market index.

Every stock and portfolio has exposures (or betas) with respect to each of these systematic risks. The pattern of economic betas for a stock or portfolio is called its *risk exposure profile*. Risk exposures are rewarded in the market with additional expected return, and thus the risk exposure profile determines the volatility *and* performance of a well-diversified portfolio. The profile also indicates how a stock or portfolio will perform under different economic conditions. For example, if real business activity is greater than anticipated, stocks with a high exposure to business activity, such as retail stores, will do relatively better than those with low exposures to business activity, such as utility companies.

Most importantly, an investment manager can control the risk exposure profile of a managed portfolio. Managers with different traditional styles, such as small-capitalization growth managers and large-capitalization value managers, have differing inherent risk exposure profiles. For this reason, a traditional manager's risk exposure profile is congruent to a particular *APT style*.

Given any particular APT style (or risk exposure profile), the difference between a manager's expected return and his or her actual performance is attributable to the selection of individual stocks that perform better or worse

---

[2] Of course, "other things equal" can only be expected to hold on average over many time periods.

than a priori expectations. This extraordinary performance defines *ex post* APT selection.

APT Equations

The APT follows from two basic postulates:

Postulate 1. In every time period, the difference between the actual (realized) return and the expected return for any asset is equal to the sum, over all risk factors, of the risk exposure (the beta for that risk factor) multiplied by the realization (the actual end-of-period value) for that risk factor, plus an asset-specific (idiosyncratic) error term.

This postulate is expressed by equation (1):

$$r_i(t) - E[r_i(t)] = \beta_{i1}f_1(t) + \ldots + \beta_{iK}f_K(t) + \varepsilon_i(t), \tag{1}$$

where

$r_i(t)$ = the total return on asset i (capital gains plus dividends) realized at the end of period t,

$E[r_i(t)]$ = the expected return, at the beginning of period t,

β_{ij} = the risk exposure or beta of asset i to risk factor j for $j = 1, \ldots, K$,

$f_j(t)$ = the value of the end-of-period realization for the jth risk factor, $j = 1, \ldots, K$, and

$\varepsilon_i(t)$ = the value of the end-of-period asset-specific (idiosyncratic) shock.

It is assumed that the expectations, at the beginning of the period, for all of the factor realizations and for the asset-specific shock are zero; that is,

$$E[f_1(t)] = \ldots = E[f_K(t)] = E[\varepsilon_i(t)] = 0.$$

It is also assumed that the asset-specific shock is uncorrelated with the factor realizations; that is,

$$\text{cov}[\varepsilon_i(t), f_j(t)] = 0 \text{ for all } j = 1, \ldots, K.$$

Finally, all of the factor realizations and the asset-specific shocks are assumed to be uncorrelated across time:

$$\text{cov}[f_j(t), f_j(t')] = \text{cov}[\varepsilon_i(t), \varepsilon_i(t')] = 0$$
$$\text{for all } j = 1, \ldots, K \text{ and for all } t \neq t'.$$

The above conditions are summarized by saying that asset returns are generated by a *linear factor model*. Note that the risk factors themselves may be correlated (inflation and interest rates, for example), as may the asset-specific shocks for different stocks (as would be the case, for example, if some unusual event influenced all of the firms in a particular industry).

Postulate 2. Pure arbitrage profits are impossible. Because of competition in financial markets, an investor cannot earn a positive expected rate of return on any combination of assets without undertaking some risk and without making some net investment of funds.

Postulate 2 is, in fact, an appealing equilibrium concept that has far-ranging implications for broad areas of financial economics well beyond the determination of asset prices. It is hard to imagine any model of financial behavior that fails to conclude that pure arbitrage profits tend to zero. This generality brings many advantages. The APT is free of restrictive assumptions on preferences or probability distributions, and it provides a rigorous logical foundation for the trade-off between expected returns and risks.

Given Postulates 1 and 2, the main APT theorem is that there exist $K + 1$ numbers $P_0, P_1, \ldots, P_K$, not all zero, such that the expected return on the ith asset is approximately equal to P_0 plus the sum over j of β_{ij} times P_j; that is,

$$E[r_i(t)] \approx P_0 + \beta_{i1}P_1 + \ldots + \beta_{iK}P_K. \tag{2}$$

Although equation (2) holds only approximately, with additional assumptions, it can be proved that it holds exactly (see, e.g., Chen and Ingersoll 1983). More importantly, even without any additional assumptions, it has been proved that the approximation in equation (2) is sufficiently accurate that any error can be ignored in practical applications (see, e.g., Dybvig 1983). Thus the approximation symbol, $\approx$, can be replaced by an equal sign:

$$E[r_i(t)] = P_0 + \beta_{i1}P_1 + \ldots + \beta_{iK}P_K. \tag{3}$$

Here, P_j is the price of risk, or the risk premium for the jth risk factor. Via equation (3), these P_j's determine the risk-return trade-off.[3]

Imagine a portfolio that is perfectly diversified (i.e., one for which $\varepsilon_p(t) = 0$) and with no factor exposures ($\beta_{pj} = 0$ for all $j = 1, \ldots, K$); such a portfolio has zero risk, and from equation (3) its expected return is P_0. Thus, P_0 must be the risk-free rate of return. Reasoning similarly, the risk premium for the jth risk

---

[3] An equivalent interpretation of equation (3) uses an analogy to the familiar relationship that "quantity $\times$ price = value." Thus, if we think of β_{ij} as the quantity of type-j risk in the ith asset and P_j as the price of type-j risk, then the product $\beta_{ij}P_j$ is the value of the contribution of type-j risk to the expected return of the ith asset. If we let V_{ij} denote this value, then it follows from equation (3) that the sum of all the values is equal to the expected excess return (the expected return in excess of the risk-free rate) for the ith asset; that is, $E[r_i(t)] - P_0 = V_{i1} + \ldots + V_{iK}$.

factor, P_j, is the return, in excess of the risk-free rate, earned on an asset that has one unit of risk exposure to the jth risk factor ($\beta_{ij} = 1$) and zero risk exposures to all of the other factors ($\beta_{ih} = 0$ for all $h \neq j$).

The full APT is obtained by substituting equation (3) into equation (1), which after rearranging terms yields:

$$r_i(t) - P_0 = \beta_{i1}[P_1 + f_1(t)] + \ldots + \beta_{iK}[P_K + f_K(t)] + \varepsilon_i(t). \qquad (4)$$

It is at this level of the determination of expected returns that the CAPM and the APT differ. In the CAPM, the expected excess return for an asset is equal to that asset's CAPM beta times the expected excess return on a market index, even for multifactor versions of the standard CAPM. For such a multifactor CAPM to be true, the APT risk premiums—the P_j's—must satisfy certain restrictions. In statistical tests, these CAPM restrictions have repeatedly been rejected in favor of the APT.

A portfolio manager controls a portfolio's betas—the portfolio's risk exposure profile—by stock selection. Note that as the risk exposure to a particular factor is, for example, increased, the expected return for that portfolio is also increased (assuming that this risk factor commands a positive risk premium). Thus, risk exposures and hence the implied expected return for a portfolio are determined by a manager's stock selection.

In many applications, data are observed monthly, and the 30-day Treasury bill rate is taken as a proxy for risk-free rate; that is, P_0 in equation (4) is replaced by $TB(t)$, the 30-day Treasury bill rate known to investors at the beginning of month t. Then, for a model with N assets ($i = 1, \ldots, N$) and a sample period of T time periods ($t = 1, \ldots, T$), the data are the asset returns, $r_i(t)$, the Treasury bill rates, $TB(t)$, and the factor realizations, $f_j(t)$. From these data, the statistical estimation problem is to obtain numerical values for the N P_j's and the ($N \times K$) β_{ij}'s. Discussion of this econometric problem is beyond the scope of this paper, but the bibliography lists further readings that cover the topic in detail.[4]

Macroeconomic Forces Impacting Stock Returns

Taking the time period to be one month and using the 30-day Treasury bill rate as a proxy for the risk-free rate of return, the APT model, equation (4), becomes:

---

[4] See, for example, Brown and Weinstein (1983); McElroy, Burmeister, and Wall (1985); Chen, Roll, and Ross (1986); Burmeister and McElroy (1988); and McElroy and Burmeister (1988).

$$r_i(t) - TB(t) = \beta_{i1}[P_1 + f_1(t)] + \ldots + \beta_{iK}[P_K + f_K(t)] + \varepsilon_i(t). \qquad (5)$$

From this point, there are three alternative approaches to estimating an APT model:

1. The risk factors $f_1(t)$, $f_2(t)$, $\ldots$, $f_K(t)$ can be computed using statistical techniques such as factor analysis or principal components.

2. K different well-diversified portfolios can substitute for the factors (see Appendix B).

3. Economic theory and knowledge of financial markets can be used to specify K risk factors that can be measured from available macroeconomic and financial data.

Each of these approaches has its merits and is appropriate for certain types of analysis. In particular, the first approach is useful for determining the number of relevant risk factors, or the numerical value of K. Many empirical studies have indicated that $K = 5$ is adequate for explaining stock returns.

The estimates extracted using factor analysis or principal components have an undesirable property, however, that renders them difficult to interpret; this problem arises because, by the nature of the technique, the estimated factors are nonunique linear combinations of more fundamental underlying economic forces. Even when these linear combinations can be given an economic interpretation, they change over time so that, for example, Factor 3 for one sample period is not necessarily the same combination—in fact, it is almost certainly different—as the combination that was Factor 3 in a different sample period.

The second approach can lead to insights, especially if the portfolios represent different strategies that are feasible for an investor to pursue at low cost. For example, if K were equal to 2, one might use small- and large-capitalization portfolios to substitute for the factors.

The advantage of the third approach is that it provides an intuitively appealing set of factors that admit economic interpretation of the risk exposures (the β_{ij}'s) and the risk premiums (the P_j's). From a purely statistical view, this approach also has the advantage of using economic information in addition to stock returns, whereas the first two approaches use "stock returns to explain stock returns." This additional information (about inflation, for example) will, in general, lead to statistical estimates with better properties, but of course, insofar as the economic variables are measured with errors, these advantages are diminished.

Selecting an appropriate set of macroeconomic factors involves almost as much art as it does science, and by now, it is a highly developed art. The practitioner requires factors that are easy to interpret, are robust over time, and explain as much as possible of the variation in stock returns. Extensive research work has established that one set of five factors meeting these criteria is the following:

- $f_1(t)$: *Confidence risk*. Confidence risk is the unanticipated changes in investors' willingness to undertake relatively risky investments. It is measured as the difference between the rate of return on relatively risky corporate bonds and the rate of return on government bonds, both with 20-year maturities, adjusted so that the mean of the difference is zero over a long historical sample period. In any month when the return on corporate bonds exceeds the return on government bonds by more than the long-run average, this measure of confidence risk is positive $(f_1 > 0)$. The intuition is that a positive return difference reflects increased investor confidence because the required yield on risky corporate bonds has fallen relative to safe government bonds. Stocks that are positively exposed to this risk $(\beta_{i1} > 0)$ then will rise in price. Most equities *do* have a positive exposure to confidence risk, and small stocks generally have greater exposure than large stocks.

- $f_2(t)$: *Time horizon risk*. Time horizon risk is the unanticipated changes in investors' desired time to payouts. It is measured as the difference between the return on 20-year government bonds and 30-day Treasury bills, again adjusted to be mean-zero over a long historical sample period. A positive realization of time horizon risk $(f_2 > 0)$ means that the price of long-term bonds has risen relative to the 30-day Treasury bill price. This is a signal that investors require less compensation for holding investments with relatively longer times to payouts. The price of stocks that are positively exposed to time horizon risk $(\beta_{i2} > 0)$ will rise to appropriately decrease their yields. Growth stocks benefit more than income stocks when this occurs.

- $f_3(t)$: *Inflation risk*. Inflation risk is a combination of the unexpected components of short- and long-run inflation rates. Expected future inflation rates are computed at the beginning of each period from available information: historical inflation rates, interest rates, and other economic variables that influence inflation. For any month, inflation risk is the unexpected surprise that is computed at the end of the month—the difference between the actual inflation for that month and what had been expected at the beginning of the month. Because most stocks have negative exposures to inflation risk $(\beta_{i3} < 0)$, a positive inflation surprise $(f_3 > 0)$ causes a negative contribution to return, whereas a negative inflation surprise $(f_3 < 0)$, a deflation shock, contributes positively toward return.

Luxury-product industries are most sensitive to inflation risk. Consumer demand for luxury goods plummets when real income is eroded through inflation, thus depressing profits for industries such as retailing, services, eating places, hotels and motels, and toys. In contrast, industries least sensitive to inflation risk tend to sell necessities, the demands for which are relatively insensitive to declines in real income. Examples include foods, cosmetics, tires and rubber goods, and shoes. Also, companies that have large asset holdings such as real estate or oil reserves may benefit from increased inflation.

- $f_4(t)$: *Business cycle risk.* Business cycle risk represents unanticipated changes in the level of real business activity. The expected values of a business activity index are computed both at the beginning and end of the month, using only information available at those times. Then, business cycle risk is calculated as the difference between the end-of-month value and the beginning-of-month value. A positive realization of business cycle risk ($f_4 > 0$) indicates that the expected growth rate of the economy, measured in constant dollars, has increased. Under such circumstances, firms that are more positively exposed to business cycle risk—for example, firms such as retail stores, which do well when business activity increases as the economy recovers from a recession—will outperform those such as utility companies that respond only weakly to increased levels in business activity.

- $f_5(t)$: *Market-timing risk.* Market-timing risk is computed as that part of the S&P 500 total return that is not explained by the first four macroeconomic risks and an intercept term. Many people find it useful to think of the APT as a generalization of the CAPM, and by including this market-timing factor, the CAPM becomes a special case. If the risk exposures to all of the first four macroeconomic factors were exactly zero (if $\beta_{i1} = \ldots = \beta_{i4} = 0$), then market-timing risk would be proportional to the S&P 500 total return. Under those extremely unlikely conditions, a stock's exposure to market-timing risk would be equal to its CAPM beta. Almost all stocks have a positive exposure to market timing risk ($\beta_{i5} > 0$), and hence positive market-timing surprises ($f_5 > 0$) increase returns, and vice versa.[5]

A natural question, then, is whether confidence risk, time horizon risk, inflation risk, and business cycle risk help to explain stock returns better than the S&P 500 alone. This question has been answered using rigorous statistical tests, and the answer is very clearly that they do.[6]

---

[5] Market-timing risk is not required in an APT model that includes *all* the relevant macroeconomic factors. As a practical matter, some relevant macroeconomic factor may be difficult to measure or may not even be observable. Market-timing risk will capture the effects of any such unobserved macroeconomic factor.

[6] The probability that the first four macroeconomic factors do not add any information that is useful for explaining stock returns is less than the probability that a standard normal variable (a

Risk Exposure Profiles and Risks—Return Trade-off

The risk exposure profile for the S&P 500 and the corresponding prices of risk (the risk premiums) are shown in Table 1.[7] For each risk factor, the contribution to expected return is the product of the risk exposure (Column 1) and the corresponding price of risk (Column 2), and the sum of these products is equal to the expected return in excess of the 30-day Treasury bill rate (Column 3). Thus, if the 30-day Treasury bill rate were, say, 5.00 percent, the forecasted return for the S&P 500 would be 5.00 + 8.09 = 13.09 percent a year.

TABLE 1. Calculation of Expected Excess Return for the S&P 500

Risk Factor	Exposure	×	Price of Risk (%/year)	=	Contribution of Risk Factor to Expected Return (%/year)
Confidence risk	0.27		2.59%		0.70%
Time horizon risk	0.56		−0.66		−0.37
Inflation risk	−0.37		−4.32		1.60
Business cycle risk	1.71		1.49		2.55
Market-timing risk	1.00		3.61		3.61
Expected excess return					8.09%

In general, then, for any asset, i, the APT risks–return trade-off defined by equation (3) is:

---

random variable that is normally distributed with a mean of zero and standard deviation of 1) exceeds 20 in value; that is, it is virtually zero. See McElroy and Burmeister (1988).

[7] The model presented in this section uses parameters estimated by the *BIRR® Risks and Returns Analyzer®* ("BIRR" is an acronym for Burmeister, Ibbotson, Roll, and Ross). The model is re-estimated every month, and the examples here and in the next sections use numbers taken from the April 1992 release, which is based on monthly data through the end of March 1992.

The *Risks and Returns Analyzer®* is a PC-based software package for doing APT-based risk analysis with a model of the sort described in this paper. Although econometric estimation of APT parameters (the risk exposures, β_{ij}'s, and the risk premiums or prices, P's) is beyond the scope of this paper, complete discussions of the more technical statistical issues involved in parameter estimation can be found in Brown and Weinstein (1983); McElroy, Burmeister, and Wall (1985); Chen, Roll, and Ross (1986); Burmeister and McElroy (1988); and McElroy and Burmeister (1988).

$$E(r_i) - TB = \beta_{i1}(2.59) + \beta_{i2}(-0.66)$$

$$+ \beta_{i3}(-4.32) + \beta_{i4}(1.49) + \beta_{i5}(3.61),$$

where TB is the 30-day Treasury bill rate. The following four observations will help clarify this risks–return trade-off:

1. The price of each risk factor determines how much expected return will change because of an increase or decrease in the portfolio's exposure to that type of risk. Suppose, for example, a well-diversified portfolio, p, has a risk exposure profile identical to that of the S&P 500, except that it has an exposure to confidence risk, β_{p1}, of 1.27 instead of 0.27 ($= \beta_{S\&P,1}$). Because the price of confidence risk (from Table 1) is 2.59 percent a year, the reward for undertaking this additional risk is 1.00 times 2.59—that is, the portfolio will have an expected return that is 2.59 percent a year higher than the expected return for the S&P 500.

2. APT risk prices can be negative, and they are for both time horizon risk and inflation risk ($P_2 < 0$ and $P_3 < 0$). Consider first inflation risk. Almost all stocks have negative exposures to inflation risk because their returns decrease with unanticipated increases in inflation. Thus, the inflation risk contribution to expected return is usually positive (the negative risk exposure times the negative price for inflation risk equals a positive contribution to expected return). That is, for most i, $\beta_{i3} < 0$, and because $P_3 < 0$, $\beta_{i3} \times P_3 > 0$ for most i.

3. Many stocks have a positive exposure to time horizon risk ($\beta_2 > 0$), however, and thus, when the price of long-term government bonds rises relative to the price of 30-day Treasury bills, their return increases. Because the reward for time horizon risk is negative ($P_2 < 0$), time horizon's contribution to the expected return for such stocks is negative; for stocks with a negative exposure to time horizon risk, its contribution is positive.

Why should this be the case? The answer is that, just as you pay for an insurance policy that pays off when your house burns down, investors desire to hold stocks with returns that increase when the relative price of long-term government bonds rises. The fact that investors want to hold stocks having this characteristic means that the prices of those stocks have been driven higher than they otherwise would have been, and therefore, their expected returns are lower. Thus, the negative price for time horizon risk produces the desired result: stocks with larger (positive) exposures to time horizon risk also have lower expected returns.

4. Table 1 is based on raw values that were not standardized.[8] A good approach for judging whether or not a particular value is significantly different from another is to plot the actual empirical distribution function across stocks and make a visual assessment. Figures 1 and 2, computed from more than 3,200 stocks in the BIRR database, illustrate this empirical distribution function for business cycle risk and the P/E, respectively.

FIGURE 1. Empirical Distribution for Business Cycle Risk (β_{i4}), Reebok and S&P 500, March 1992

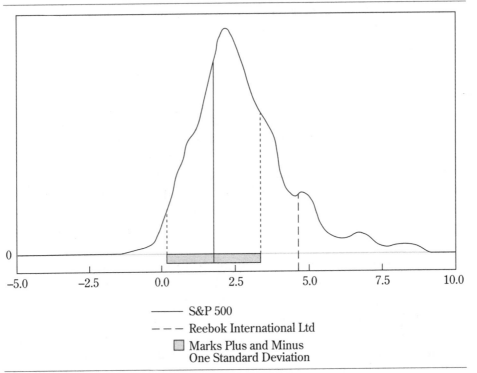

— S&P 500

– – – Reebok International Ltd

☐ Marks Plus and Minus One Standard Deviation

Source: BIRR Portfolio Analysis, Inc.

[8] It is not uncommon for the numerical values of financial attributes (such as P/E's) to be reported in units of standard deviation. A standardized value is computed by first transforming the variable so that it has a mean of zero and unit variance; a standardized value of 1.0 (-1.0) means that the value lies one standard deviation above (below) the mean. Provided the attribute is distributed normally, 68.26 percent of the observations lie between the standardized values -1.0 and 1.0, 95.44 percent lie between -2.0 and 2.0, and so forth. Such standardized values can be

FIGURE 2. **Empirical Distribution for Price–Earnings Ratios, Low-P/E Stocks and S&P 500, March 1992**

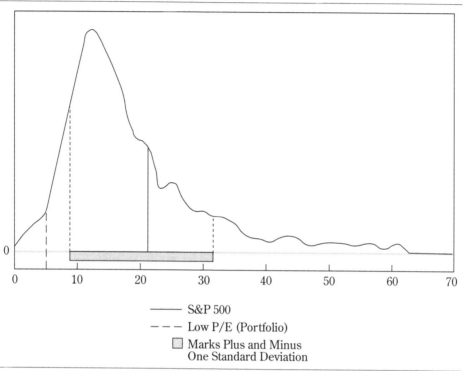

Source: BIRR Portfolio Analysis, Inc.
Note: Low-P/E firms are represented by a value-weighted portfolio of the 50 lowest P/E stocks listed on the NYSE.

In Figure 1, the empirical distribution for business cycle risk, β_{i4}, for i = the S&P 500 is indicated by the solid vertical line and the β_{i4} for i = Reebok International Ltd. is indicated by the vertical dashed line. The box on the horizontal axis centered on the S&P 500 line indicates plus and minus one standard deviation of business cycle risk for all the stocks in the database—that is, the width of the box is two standard deviations for the across-firm distribution. Note that the distribution does not appear normal.

In Figure 2, the P/E for the S&P 500 is indicated by the solid line and the P/E for a market-value-weighted portfolio of the 50 lowest P/E stocks listed on the

misleading, however, and even dangerous if the underlying financial attribute is not distributed normally.

13

New York Stock Exchange is indicated by the vertical dashed line. Again, note that the distribution is not normal and appears to be skewed to the right.

As is evident from Figure 1, the business cycle risk for Reebok is much larger than for the S&P 500. These risk exposure profiles are shown below.

	Exposure for Reebok	*Exposure for S&P 500*
Confidence Risk	0.73	0.27
Time Horizon Risk	0.77	0.56
Inflation Risk	−0.48	−0.37
Business Cycle Risk	4.59	1.71
Market-Timing Risk	1.50	1.00

These exposures give rise to an expected excess rate of return for Reebok equal to 15.71 percent a year, compared with the 8.09 percent a year computed for the S&P 500. Figure 3 compares the risk exposure profiles for Reebok and the S&P 500.[9]

In general, the risk exposure profiles of individual stocks and of portfolios can differ significantly. For example, Figures 4, 5, 6, and 7 compare the respective risk exposure profiles for portfolios of low-capitalization versus high-capitalization stocks, growth stocks versus the S&P 500, a value portfolio versus the BIRR stock database, and a growth versus high-yield portfolio. These risk exposure profiles define APT styles, and they enable us to view traditional portfolio management styles from a new perspective that reveals their inherent macroeconomic risks.

The usefulness to practitioners of risk exposure profiles and the risk–return trade-off is an empirical issue. Abundant evidence shows that market indexes are not mean–variance efficient; if so, the usual implementations of the CAPM using some market index as a proxy are invalid. More importantly, recent empirical evidence demonstrates that CAPM betas do not accurately explain returns.

The multifactor APT approach has far greater explanatory power than the CAPM. Many econometric studies have verified the superior performance of models that include multiple factors (Postulate 1 of the APT) to explain returns and that use multiple factor premiums (Postulate 2 of the APT) to explain expected returns. These results are discussed in some of the papers listed in

---

[9] The BIRR Risk Index plotted in this and the following graphs is a single number that gives an approximate answer to the question, "Does A have more systematic risk, relative to the market, than B?"

FIGURE 3. Risk Exposure Profiles for Reebok and the S&P 500, March 1992

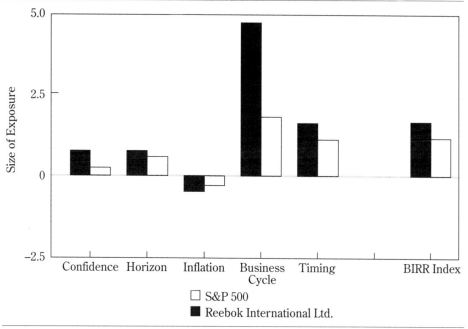

Source: BIRR Portfolio Analysis, Inc.

the bibliography, especially Roll and Ross (1980), Burmeister and McElroy (1988), McElroy and Burmeister (1988), and Fama and French (1992).

Contribution to Return from Macroeconomic Surprises

No matter how precise the model of expected return, surprises always occur, and expected returns differ from actual returns. Taking expectations of equation (5), it follows that the expected return for the ith asset in period t is given by

$$E[r_i(t)] = TB(t) + \beta_{i1}P_1 + \ldots + \beta_{iK}P_K. \qquad (6)$$

The expected return given by equation (6) is rarely equal to the actual return. Because factors seldom do exactly what is forecast for them and because the idiosyncratic portion of return, $\varepsilon_i(t)$, is almost never zero, the actual return for the ith asset is

$$r_i(t) = E[r_i(t)] + U[r_i(t)], \qquad (7)$$

where $U[r_i(t)]$ is the unexpected return given by

FIGURE 4. Risk Exposure Profiles for Market-Value-Weighted Portfolios of the 50 Lowest and Highest Capitalization Stocks listed on the NYSE, March 1992

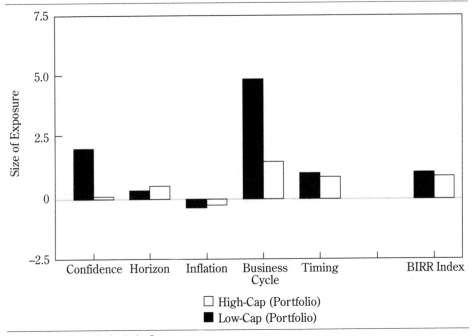

Source: BIRR Portfolio Analysis, Inc.

$$U[r_i(t)] = \beta_{i1}f_1(t) + \ldots + \beta_{iK}f_K(t) + \varepsilon_i(t). \tag{8}$$

Suppose now we consider a historical sample period $t = 1, \ldots, T$ and let bars denote sample period means. The mean *ex post* actual return for the ith asset is

$$\bar{r}_i = \bar{E}(r_i) + \bar{U}(r_i)$$
$$= \bar{E}(r_i) + \beta_{i1}\bar{f}_1 + \ldots + \beta_{iK}\bar{f}_K + \bar{\varepsilon}_i. \tag{9}$$

That is, the historical mean return for the ith asset is equal to the sum of the mean *ex post* expected return and the mean of the surprise components of return.

The mean *ex post* unexpected macroeconomic factor return is

$$\beta_{i1}\bar{f}_1 + \ldots + \beta_{iK}\bar{f}_K,$$

and the *ex post* sample period alpha for the ith asset is

FIGURE 5. **Risk Exposure Profiles for a Market-Value-Weighted Portfolio of the 50 Highest Growth Stocks Listed on the NYSE and for the S&P 500, March 1992**

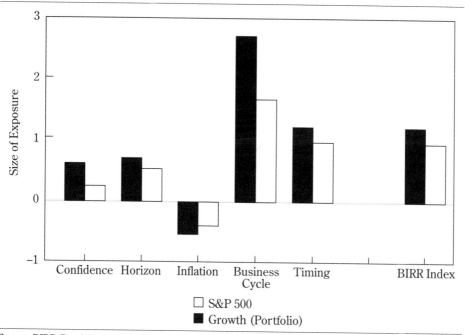

Source: BIRR Portfolio Analysis, Inc.

$$\alpha_i \equiv \bar{\varepsilon}_i.$$

Putting all this together, for the ith asset, the mean *ex post* actual return is equal to the mean *ex post* expected return plus the mean *ex post* unexpected macroeconomic factor return plus α_i. The first term on the right side of this equality measures the rewards for risks; it is the reward a manager receives that is attributable to the risk exposure profile for the portfolio. The second term has two possible interpretations: (1) If a manager has taken intentional macroeconomic bets (e.g., a "bet" on an economic expansion through an unusually large exposure to business cycle risk), the unexpected macroeconomic factor return measures the success or failure of those bets; but (2) if a manager is not intentionally making factor bets, the unexpected return can be interpreted simply as a measure of good or bad luck in this sample period. The last term, α_i, is a measure of a manager's selection of individual stocks that perform better or worse than a priori expectations and is the measure of APT selection.

FIGURE 6. **Risk Exposure Profiles for a Market-Value-Weighted Portfolio of the 50 Lowest P/E Stocks among the 500 Largest NYSE Firms and for an Equal-Weighted Portfolio of All Stocks in the BIRR Data Base, March 1992**

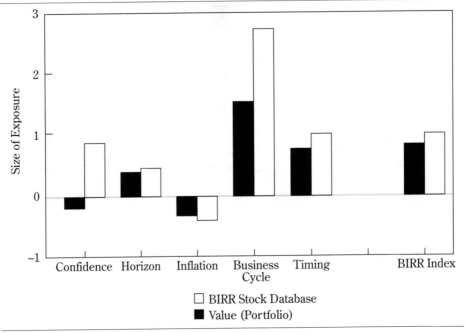

Source: BIRR Portfolio Analysis, Inc.

By construction, all of the macroeconomic factors have zero population means (they have zero-mean probability distributions), so over long historical periods, their sample means will be approximately zero. Thus, over long historical sample periods, the contribution to return from macroeconomic surprises will be approximately zero.[10] Over long time periods, then, almost all of the mean realized return will be rewards for risks and, possibly, APT selection.

---

[10] This statement is literally true for a portfolio with constant betas. It is possible, however, that "timing" managers can successfully alter betas from period to period so that the average contribution of the factor surprises to portfolio returns is *not* zero. For instance, if managers can predict changes in real business activity (as measured, say, by industrial production) better than the market as a whole, they could structure their portfolios to have high (low) business cycle exposure when they predict an increase (decrease) in business activity.

FIGURE 7. **Risk Exposure Profiles for a Growth Portfolio and for a Market-Value-Weighted Portfolio of the 50 Highest Dividend Yield NYSE Stocks, March 1992**

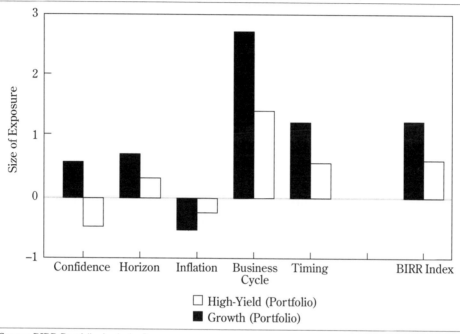

Source: BIRR Portfolio Analysis, Inc.
Note: The growth portfolio is as described in Figure 5.

Over short time periods, this will not be the case, even for managers with timing skills; the surprises arising from the macroeconomic factors can have significant impacts on realized returns, as Table 2 shows for Reebok and the S&P 500.

TABLE 2. **Annual Mean *Ex Post* Unexpected Macroeconomic Factor Return, Reebok and S&P 500**

Sample Period	Reebok	S&P 500
4/91–3/92 (12 months)	−2.03%	−1.58%
10/90–3/92 (18 months)	14.24	9.31
4/90–3/92 (24 months)	−0.95	−0.86
4/87–3/92 (60 months)	−4.01	−2.95
4/86–3/92 (72 months)	−0.26	−0.56

How to Use the APT: Some Examples

A primary concern for practitioners is not only to acquire an understanding of the APT but also to learn how to use it to enhance their investment performance. So far, we have concentrated on explaining the APT; now, we will briefly discuss several uses of the APT that every practitioner could easily apply. The following list is chosen to be exemplary of some widely used APT techniques, but it is by no means exhaustive.

Evaluation of Macroeconomic Risk Exposures and Attribution of Return.

Risk exposure profiles can vary widely for stocks and portfolios. They are determined by the risks a manager undertakes through stock selection, and in turn, determine a manager's APT style. A basic first task, then, is to identify the risk exposure profiles for portfolios. Usually, managers will want to compare their risk exposure profiles with those for appropriate benchmarks. A small-cap manager, for example, should know whether his or her portfolio differs in its exposure to macroeconomic risks from an appropriate index of small-cap firms. Any differences will account for performance differentials from the index. Only if the risk exposures are the same as the index can *ex post* superior performance be attributed to APT selection—selection of individual stocks that returned more than would be expected on the basis of the risks undertaken.

Whatever the manager's risk exposure profile, the APT should be used to divide the mean *ex post* actual return into: (1) expected return, which is the reward for the risks taken, (2) unexpected macroeconomic factor return, which arises from factor bets and factor surprises, and (3) α, which arises from stock selection. Moreover, expected and unexpected factor return can be attributed to the manager's risk exposure profile. Thus, APT analysis will provide a better understanding of the true sources of actual portfolio performance.

Index Portfolios.

A closely related use of the APT is in the formation of index portfolios designed to track particular well-diversified benchmarks. The APT provides powerful tools for tracking any such benchmark portfolio. A tracking portfolio can be constructed simply by forming a portfolio with a matching risk exposure profile. The *ex post* APT α can be made small by making the tracking portfolio well diversified so that the portfolio-specific return, call it ε_p, is near zero.

Tracking a benchmark that itself is not well diversified, in the sense that its *ex post* α usually is not near zero, is more difficult. In this case, not only the risk exposure profiles but also the benchmark's α must be matched. One way to do this is to form the tracking portfolio by random sampling from the stocks that constitute the benchmark.

Tilting, or Making a Factor Bet. Good managers may possess superior knowledge about the economy. Suppose, for example, a manager believes that the economy is going to recover from a recession faster than most market participants do. If the manager is correct in this belief, the realizations of business cycle risk will be positive ($f_4 > 0$), and stocks that have greater risk exposures to business cycle risk (stocks for which β_{i4} is larger) will, *ceteris paribus*, outperform.

To take advantage of this superior knowledge, the manager will want to make a factor bet on (or tilt toward) business cycle risk—alter the existing portfolio to increase its business cycle risk exposure without changing any other macroeconomic risks. Conversely, if a manager has special knowledge that the economy is going to slide into a recession, he or she will want to lower the portfolio's exposure to business cycle risk.

Multimanager Fund Performance. Most sponsors employ more than one manager. Even though each may perform well when compared with a particular style benchmark, that is not the issue of most importance to a sponsor. A sponsor wants to evaluate the risks and performance of the overall fund.

The sponsor should combine the portfolios of individual managers into one overall fund portfolio and then use the APT to examine the risk exposure profile and performance of the fund portfolio. Often, the combination of managers leads to risk exposures that the sponsor finds uncomfortable. If so, funds should be reallocated among the managers to achieve the desired fund risk exposure profile.

The sponsor must also examine whether or not the overall fund return exceeds the benchmark and determine the sources of differences.

Optimized Risk Control with Manager-Supplied Rankings. Many managers have their own proprietary methods for evaluating stock return performance, yet lack adequate methods for estimating their accompanying risks. The APT, or more accurately, part of the APT, is a perfect tool for such managers.

To keep matters simple, suppose a manager has a personal ranking system that scores every stock on a scale from 1 to 10, where 10 is the score given to the stocks in the best expected return category. The objective is to emulate the volatility of the S&P 500 but achieve a higher return. How could the manager use the APT?

Let s_i be the score from 1 to 10 assigned to the ith stock ($i = 1, \ldots, N$). The formal problem is to find portfolio weights, $w_1, w_2, \ldots, w_N$, for the N stocks in the selection universe such that the portfolio score is maximized but the risk exposure profile is similar to that of the S&P 500. More formally, the weights should result in the highest possible value for

$$w_1 \times s_1 + w_2 \times s_2 + \ldots + w_N \times s_N,$$

subject to the constraint that the portfolio betas,

$$\beta_{pj} = w_1 \times \beta_{1j} + w_2 \times \beta_{2j} + \ldots + w_N \times \beta_{Nj}$$

for $j = 1, \ldots, K$, are close to the betas for the S&P 500. That is, the weights should make the risk exposure profile for the portfolio close to the risk exposure profile for the S&P 500 while maximizing the value of the portfolio's ranking score. If the ranking system works, the return will be superior to the S&P 500. If the resulting portfolio is well-diversified, it and the S&P 500 will have approximately equal volatilities. The proper diversification can be achieved by making N sufficiently large and by imposing a maximum value for the weights so that the portfolio contains a large number of stocks. This optimization problem is easily solved using linear programming.

Long–Short Investment Strategies. Long–short, or market-neutral, investment strategies are receiving increased attention. The pure APT view of such strategies will be discussed first; then, it will be shown how managers with superior knowledge can use the APT to implement those strategies effectively.

Suppose a manager holds a long portfolio with return $r_L(t)$ and a short portfolio with return $r_S(t)$; both have equal dollar values. Let the risk exposures for these portfolios be denoted by β_{Lj} and β_{Sj}, $j = 1, \ldots, K$. Assuming that the short position earns the 30-day Treasury bill rate, the manager's total return is

$$r_L(t) - r_S(t) + TB(t).$$

Now, let the risk exposure profile on the long portfolio exactly match the risk exposure profile on the short position. Then, using equation (3), the *expected* returns on the long and short portfolios are equal, the expected return to the long–short strategy is simply $TB(t)$, and the variance of the realized return is

$$var[\varepsilon_L(t) - \varepsilon_S(t) + TB(t)].$$

Because no stock is held in both the long and short portfolios, this variance is approximately

$$\text{var}[\varepsilon_L(t)] + \text{var}[\varepsilon_S(t)] + \text{var}[TB(t)].$$

The position has greater volatility than 30-day Treasury bills but no greater mean return. Therefore, it is not a very attractive strategy, particularly after trading costs.

This strategy could become attractive if the APT alphas on the long position were significantly larger than the APT alphas on the short position; that is, it is an attractive strategy for a manager with superior APT selection. Consider an exceptional manager who can pick two well-diversified portfolios of stocks, with no stocks in common, such that $\alpha_L > 0$ for the long portfolio and $\alpha_S < 0$ for the short portfolio. If the manager also can match the risk exposure profiles of the long and short positions, the return would be $\alpha_L - \alpha_S + TB(t)$ with a volatility approximately equal to that of 30-day Treasury bills.

The APT can play a crucial role for such a manager: It provides an easy and quick way to match the risk exposure profiles of the long and short positions. As an example of this role of the APT, we constructed a long portfolio consisting of approximately 50 NYSE-listed stocks with the largest *ex post* alphas over a sample period of 72 months (April 1986 to March 1992). We then computed the risk exposure profile for this long portfolio. A short portfolio of approximately 50 NYSE-listed stocks, not in the long portfolio, was also selected. An optimization problem was solved to find portfolio weights for the short position that matched its risk exposure profile to that of the long position. The resulting risk exposure profile for the overall long–short strategy is illustrated in Figure 8; it has essentially zero systematic risk. The sole source of volatility (beyond the volatility of 30-day Treasury bills) for this long–short strategy comes from the ε's for the long and short positions. By having portfolios of 50 stocks or more, this volatility can be kept small.

The performance of this long–short, or market-neutral, strategy for the most recent 12 months of the sample period (April 1991 to March 1992) is illustrated in Figure 9. The mean realized return was 30.04 percent a year, compared with 11.57 percent for the S&P 500, and the standard deviation of this realized return was only 6.26 percent a year, compared with 18.08 percent for the S&P 500.

Mean–Variance Efficiency. The standard optimization problem of finding the portfolio with the highest expected rate of return for a given variance is easily solved within an APT framework. For this problem, the expected return could either be given by the APT equation, equation (3), or it could come

FIGURE 8. **Risk Exposure Profile for the Market-Neutral Strategy and for the S&P 500**

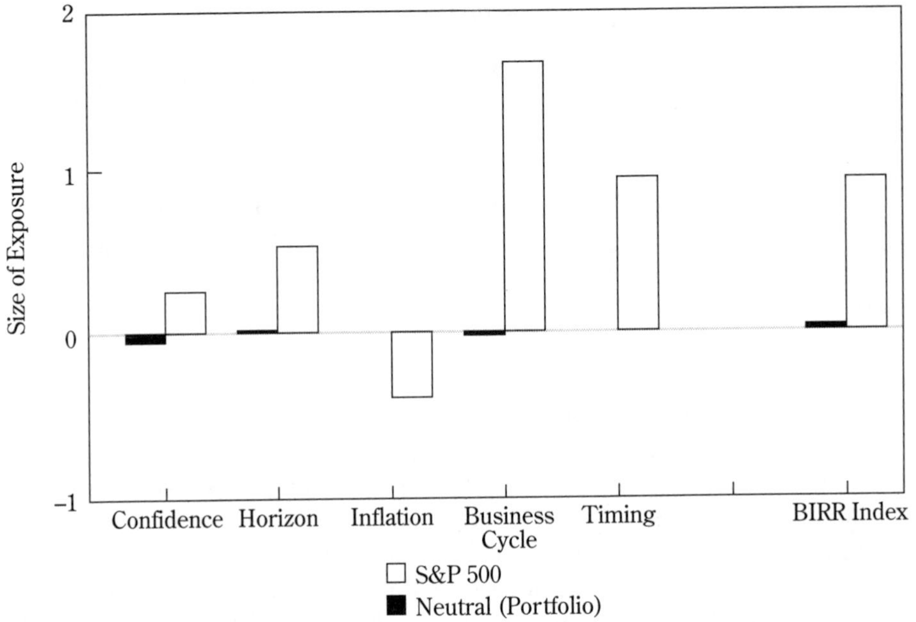

Source: BIRR Portfolio Analysis, Inc.
Note: The risk profile values for the market-neutral strategy are as follows: confidence risk = −0.02, time horizon risk = 0.02, inflation risk = 0.00, business cycle risk = −0.02, and market-timing risk = 0.00; the BIRR risk index = 0.01.

from manager-supplied rankings. In either case, a variety of computational methods can be used to calculate the optimal portfolio weights. In such problems, one often takes the APT's systematic variance (rather than total variance) as given and then imposes constraints to assure that the resulting portfolio is well diversified. This procedure often produces superior results because estimates of stock return variances and, especially, covariances tend to have large out-of-sample errors.

Conclusion

What we have described in this paper is the foundation for the more sophisticated portfolio management techniques that the APT makes possible. Our hope is that a careful reading will enable practitioners to apply the APT to

FIGURE 9.   Cumulative Wealth, Market-Neutral Strategy and the S&P 500

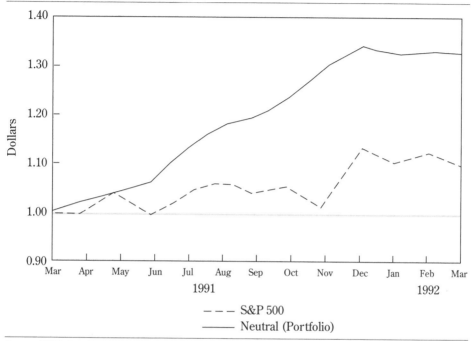

Source: BIRR Portfolio Analysis, Inc.

the construction of superior portfolios and will help provide an understanding of the true sources of actual risks and returns. In contrast to other common return measurement approaches, the APT offers fewer explanations for return differences. This simplicity is a great virtue. Understanding the true sources of stock returns is much easier with an APT model than with models having dozens and dozens of parameters that supposedly influence returns.

The basic APT model described here can be enhanced in many ways. Some of the generalizations now in use include the following:

- Allowing the risk prices, P_j's, to vary over time.
- Allowing the risk exposures, the β_{ij}'s, to vary over time.
- Using Bayesian methods to produce optimal out-of-sample forecasts for the risk exposures and hence for the expected returns.
- Introducing additional factors with zero-risk prices, which are typically used to capture industry and sector effects. Although such nonpriced

25

factors do not contribute to expected return, they do help to explain volatility, and they provide managers with a tool to evaluate the diversification of their portfolios.

Other enhancements are being invented every day. As more and more tools become available and as understanding of the APT spreads, so does its application to portfolio management problems.

Appendix A

To derive the restrictions that a multifactor CAPM must obey, suppose that the CAPM were true for some market index of N assets. This index has a return denoted by $r_m(t)$ and has weights $w_{m1}, w_{m2}, \ldots, w_{mN}$ summing to 1. Suppose also that Postulate 1 of the APT holds, that is, that the N asset returns are generated by the linear factor model (LFM) given in equation (1). We will then show that the APT is valid and find the CAPM restrictions that the APT risk prices must satisfy.

This problem is solved by recognizing that the CAPM beta for any asset can be computed as a linear function of the LFM risk exposures; that is, the CAPM beta is equal to a linear function of the APT β_{ij}'s.

First note that the return on the market index is

$$r_m(t) = w_{m1} \times r_1(t) + \ldots + w_{mN} \times r_N(t)$$

and hence is generated by a LFM with

$$\beta_{mj} = w_{m1} \times \beta_{1j} + \ldots + w_{mN} \times \beta_{Nj} \text{ for } j = 1, \ldots, K.$$

Using Footnote 1, the CAPM beta for the ith asset is

$$\beta_i = \frac{\text{cov}[r_i(t), r_m(t)]}{\text{var}[r_m(t)]}.$$

The latter can be computed from the LFM generating the return for the ith asset:

$$\beta_i = \frac{\beta_{i1} \times \text{cov}[f_1(t), r_m(t)]}{\text{var}[r_m(t)]} + \ldots$$

$$+ \frac{\beta_{iK} \times \text{cov}[f_K(t), r_m(t)]}{\text{var}[r_m(t)]}$$

$$+ \frac{\text{cov}[\varepsilon_i(t), r_m(t)]}{\text{var}[r_m(t)]}.$$

Because by Postulate 1 $\text{cov}[\varepsilon_i(t), f_j(t)] = 0$, it follows that $\text{cov}[\varepsilon_i(t), r_m(t)] = \text{cov}[\varepsilon_i(t), \varepsilon_m(t)]$. Thus, under the usual assumption that the market index is well diversified and $\varepsilon_m(t)$ is approximately zero, we may set the last covariance term in the above expression for β_i equal to zero.

Under the CAPM, $E[r_i(t) - TB(t)] = \beta_i \times E[r_m(t) - TB(t)]$. The APT is true when there exist numbers $P_1, \ldots, P_K$ such that

$$E[r_i(t) - TB(t)] = \beta_{i1} \times P_1 + \ldots + \beta_{iK} \times P_K.$$

It then follows immediately that the APT holds provided that

$$P_j = \frac{\text{cov}[f_j(t), r_m(t)] \times E[r_m(t) - TB(t)]}{\text{var}[r_m(t)]}$$

for all $j = 1, \ldots, K$. Conversely, if the APT is true and the above K CAPM restrictions on the P_j's hold, then the CAPM is also true. Given an LFM for asset returns, these are the CAPM restrictions that are rejected in favor of the APT in statistical tests.

Appendix B

We will show that K well-diversified portfolios can substitute for the factors in an APT model. To simplify the computations, we assume that $K = 2$; the general case is easily handled using matrix algebra. Thus, suppose that two different well-diversified portfolios have returns given by

$$R_1(t) = TB(t) + \beta_{11}[P_1 + f_1(t)] + \beta_{12}[P_2 + f_2(t)] + \varepsilon_1(t)$$

and

$$R_2(t) = TB(t) + \beta_{21}[P_1 + f_1(t)] + \beta_{22}[P_2 + f_2(t)] + \varepsilon_2(t).$$

Also assume that the risk exposure profiles for the two portfolios are not proportional. We will show below that
  (a) The APT equation for the return on the ith asset, $r_i(t)$, given by equation (5), can be rewritten in terms of the portfolios with returns $R_1(t)$ and $R_2(t)$.
  (b) Given the answer to (a), $E[r_i(t)]$ can be expressed in terms of the expected returns for the two portfolios.
To prove (a) and (b), we introduce the following simplifying notation:

$$y_1(t) \equiv R_1(t) - TB(t) - \varepsilon_1(t),$$
$$y_2(t) \equiv R_2(t) - TB(t) - \varepsilon_2(t),$$
$$z_1(t) \equiv [P_1 + f_1(t)], \text{ and}$$
$$z_2(t) \equiv [P_2 + f_2(t)].$$

In this notation, the APT equations for the two portfolios are

$$y_1(t) = \beta_{11}z_1(t) + \beta_{12}z_2(t)$$

and

$$y_2(t) = \beta_{21}z_1(t) + \beta_{22}z_2(t).$$

Taking $y_1(t)$ and $y_2(t)$ as given, the latter are two equations in two unknown z's, and they may be solved for

$$z_1(t) = b_{11}y_1(t) + b_{12}y_2(t)$$

and

$$z_2(t) = b_{21}y_1(t) + b_{22}y_2(t),$$

where

$$b_{11} = \beta_{22}/\delta,$$
$$b_{12} = -\beta_{12}/\delta,$$
$$b_{21} = -\beta_{21}/\delta,$$
$$b_{22} = \beta_{11}/\delta,$$

and

$$\delta = (\beta_{11}\beta_{22} - \beta_{12}\beta_{21}).$$

Note that as long as the risk exposure profiles for the two portfolios are not proportional, $\delta \neq 0$ and the solution given above exists.

Given these results, with straightforward algebraic manipulation, equation (5) may be rewritten as

$$r_i(t) - TB(t) = c_{i1}[R_1(t) - TB(t)] + c_{i2}[R_2(t) - TB(t)] + e_i(t),$$

where

$$c_{i1} = \beta_{i1}b_{11} + \beta_{i2}b_{21},$$
$$c_{i2} = \beta_{i1}b_{12} + \beta_{i2}b_{22},$$

and

$$e_i(t) = \varepsilon_i(t) - c_{i1}\varepsilon_1(t) - c_{i2}\varepsilon_2(t).$$

This exercise establishes (a) above.

Finally, taking expectations of the latter equation gives

$$E[r_i(t) - TB(t)] = c_{i1}E[R_1(t) - TB(t)] + c_{i2}E[R_2(t) - TB(t)] + 0.$$

This formulation proves (b) above.

Multi-Index Models Using Simultaneous Estimation of all Parameters

Edwin J. Elton
Martin J. Gruber
Leonard N. Stern School of Business
New York University

The concept of index models and their role in explaining and understanding the pattern of security returns, what affects individual security returns, the selection of optimal portfolios, and the level of relative long-run (equilibrium) returns have been widely discussed. We will review these techniques as an introduction to the concepts of estimating multi-index models.

Single- vs. Multi-Index Models

Most of our analysis will be in the context of a generic multi-index model and a generic single-index model. The single-index model is included because it is familiar and because it serves as a useful benchmark against which to judge multi-index models. In addition, many of the problems with the multi-index model, and the economic intuitions behind the solution to those problems, can be illustrated for the case of a single-index model.

The single-index model is simply a way of decomposing return on an asset into two parts. The first part, the systematic part, is the portion of return affected by influences common to all assets. The second part is the unsystematic part, which is assumed to be unique to the asset. Thus,

$$\begin{pmatrix} Return \\ on \\ Asset \end{pmatrix} = \begin{pmatrix} Systematic \\ Part \end{pmatrix} + \begin{pmatrix} Unique \\ Part \end{pmatrix},$$

or

$$R_{it} = (b_{i1}f_{1t}) + (\alpha_i + e_{it}), \tag{1}$$

where

R_{it} = is the return on security i in time t,
b_{i1} = is the sensitivity of security i to returns on Index 1,
f_{1t} = is the return on Index 1 in period t,
α_i = is the expected level of nonindex-related return for security i, and
e_{it} = is a random variable with mean of zero and variance $\sigma^2_{e_{it}}$.

Note that the unique return is also split into two parts: its mean level, α_i, and its variability, e_{it}. For the single-index model to be a reasonable description of reality, the unique part should be truly unique to the security in question and not related to another influence. Technically, this means that the value of the unique return for security i in period t is unrelated to the value for security j in period t. Because the α's are constants, this condition means

$$E(e_{it}e_{jt}) = 0 \text{ for all } i \text{ and } j, \text{ where } i \neq j.$$

Likewise, for the researcher to have correctly divided the return into its systematic and unique parts, the unique return must be unrelated to the index return so that

$$E(e_{it}f_{1t}) = 0 \text{ for all securities.}$$

The single-index model describes return in terms of one common influence, and the multi-index model describes returns in terms of more than one common influence. Its structure is exactly the same as that of the single-index model except for the inclusion of additional indexes. Thus, the model can be written as

$$R_{it} = \alpha_i + b_{i1}f_{1t} + b_{i2}f_{2t} + \ldots + b_{ij}f_{jt} + e_{it}, \tag{2}$$

where

f_{jt} = the return on the jth index affecting stock return, and
b_{ij} = the sensitivity of security i to the jth index.

As in the single-index case, unique return is assumed to be uncorrelated across all securities; that is,

$$E(e_{it}e_{jt}) = 0 \text{ for all } i \text{ and all } j, \text{ where } i \neq j,$$

and systematic influences are assumed to be independent of unique influences:[1]

$$E(e_{it}f_{jt}) = 0 \text{ for all } i \text{ and all } j.$$

The major reason for going to a multi-index model is the belief that influences beyond one index cause securities to be correlated with each other (move together). In fact, additional indexes are introduced in an attempt to have the e_{it} be the unique influence so the covariance between the residuals in equation (2) will be approximately zero. This attempt to find a set of indexes that captures all significant influences that affect multiple securities results in an approximate zero covariance between residuals that will be the key to designing a multi-index model.

To this point, we have intentionally defined our analysis in the terminology of multi-index models. Historically, starting with Sharpe's single-index model, this terminology was commonly used both in the literature and practice of financial analysts. With Ross's (1976) description of the arbitrage pricing theory (APT) and the initial tests of Roll and Ross (1980) of the APT methodology, a different terminology came into existence. Expressions like equation (2) became known as a multi-factor return-generating process. The f_j, which we denoted as returns on indexes, became known as factors, and the b_{ij} became factor loadings.

Estimating the Multi-Index Model

To use a multi-factor (multi-index) model, we need to estimate the right-hand side of equation (2). We need estimates of both the f_j factors and the factor loadings, b_{ij}. Either the f_j or the b_{ij} can be asserted on a priori grounds with the other identified empirically, or both can be identified empirically.

Clearly, estimating one set of parameters should be easier than estimating both sets simultaneously, but we do not do so because we do not know what the correct set is. We can illustrate this problem with the case of the single-index model. Usually, when estimating a single-index model, the index is taken to be the return or excess return (over the riskless rate) on some widely diversified portfolio. The most commonly used portfolios are the S&P 500 Index or the CRSP Index. One of these is simply asserted as being the relevant factor.

If the Sharpe–Lintner version of the CAPM is correct, the right index to use

---

[1] An additional assumption that is frequently made is that the indexes are uncorrelated. This assumption does not create problems, because a set of correlated indexes can always be converted to a set of uncorrelated indexes.

for explaining equilibrium returns is an index of the return on all risky assets in which the weight on each return is the relevant market proportion of that asset.

If the model is not correct, there is no theoretical way of identifying an appropriate index and the definition of the relevant index is not clear-cut. Furthermore, even if the standard CAPM is a relevant equilibrium model, no one would be able to calculate the return on a market-weighted index of all assets. Although a market-weighted index of equities is readily available, market-weighted indexes of other assets, such as real estate, are not. Plausibly, a non-market-weighted index of equities (one that places greater weight on equities correlated with excluded assets such as real estate) could be a better representation of the true "market" index than is a market-weighted index of equities alone.

If we feel a multi-index model better represents the return structure, the problems become more severe. No theoretical multi-index equilibrium model is generally accepted. Although alternative theory suggests certain broad influences that might affect equilibrium returns, these influences are not easily translated into empirically measurable influences.

An alternative to prespecifying indexes is to try to have the historical return series itself suggest what portfolios of securities would best serve as indexes. Equation (1) and its explanation suggest the characteristics these indexes should possess. In particular, they should separate the common influences in returns from the unique influences in returns. After we have specified the indexes, the unique returns on securities should be uncorrelated with each other. In addition, the structure should be parsimonious; that is, returns can be described in terms of a limited number of indexes. Finally, having the indexes represent separate influences would be desirable.

Two statistical techniques accomplish these goals: factor analysis and principal components analysis.[2] The most common technique is factor analysis. Factor analysis was devised to define a set of indexes mathematically so that the covariance between security returns is minimized after the indexes have been removed. This assures that $\text{cov}(e_i e_j)$ is as close to zero as it can be.

More precisely, once the user sets the number of indexes desired, factor analysis will:

- Define the optimal composition of each index (the weight on each security in each index),

---

[2] See the appendix to this chapter for a more detailed discussion of factor analysis and principal components analysis, as well as the differences between them.

- Specify the return of each index at each point in time (this is the same concept as the return of the S&P Index at each point in time),
- Calculate the b_{ij}, or sensitivity of each stock to each index, and
- Measure the average explanatory power of the model for each stock.

One can then repeat the analysis for a different number of factors (indexes) and determine the probability of needing to add another factor to the model.

Design Issues

Although the idea of letting the data design the model has a lot of appeal, in statistical methodology, as in economics, there are few free lunches. The techniques come with their own problems and their own set of choices. We will discuss four of these: the effect of the choice of data, the number of indexes to use, indeterminacy of the model, and computational difficulties.

The Choice of Data. The input to factor or principal component analysis is a sample of security returns. In preparing the return data, the researcher must select both the time period of returns and the sample of stocks (or portfolios of stocks) to use to estimate a factor structure. Ideally, the structure will hold for time periods and securities beyond those used in the estimation sample.

Obviously, the data cannot suggest a factor if that factor was not present during the time period chosen. For example, assume that changes in oil prices affect equity returns. Using returns from a period with minimal changes in oil prices will probably mean that changes in oil prices had a very small influence on security returns in the period and that this factor will not be recovered by factor analysis. Similarly, if the researcher selected a sample of stocks that happened to have only a few stocks that are sensitive to changes in oil prices, the influence of oil prices would not show up as a factor.

Researchers frequently attempt to mitigate computational problems by factor analyzing the returns on portfolios of securities rather than returns on individual securities. This technique can introduce other problems into the analysis. For example, when factor analyzing a time series of returns, generally the first index is a portfolio of most of the assets whose returns are being factor analyzed and the sensitivity of all assets to the index is positive. This is not true with subsequent indexes, however. Additional indexes generally measure nonmarket influences. For example, it is not uncommon when factor analyzing equity returns that the second index is highly correlated with firm capitalization (captures the small-stock phenomenon) with the effect of the market removed. Some securities will have positive sensitivities to the influence of size and others negative. The sensitivities on a portfolio of securities is a weighted average of the sensitivities of the securities that compose it. If some sensitivities are positive and some negative, the portfolio's sensitivity could be zero or close to zero. Factor analyzing returns at the portfolio level could mean that important influences would not be detected.

The Number of Indexes. A second design issue that affects results is the number of indexes in the return-generating process. The factor analytic techniques specify, for a fixed number of indexes, the indexes that best separate out common influences from unique influences. Although statistical techniques can determine whether adding another influence "statistically" improves the explanatory power of the model, common sense and economic significance play a major role in deciding on the number of factors to analyze. For example, does the composition of the last index make intuitive sense in terms of capturing an influence the analyst feels might affect security prices. For testing economic significance, the analyst will examine such issues as whether the index improves the ability to construct portfolios that match a market index and whether the index helps explain the time series of security returns in a period other than when the model was fit.

The Nonuniqueness of Factors. A third design issue is concerned with the indeterminacy of the structure of the multi-index model.[3] An infinite number of models can separate returns into systematic and nonsystematic components. For example, consider the single-index model, and assume the index is the return on the S&P Index. In a second model, the index is half the return of the S&P Index and all the sensitivities are doubled, but the result is the same separation of return into systematic and unsystematic parts.

Multi-index models become even more complex. An infinite number of specifications will result in the same separation of systematic and unsystematic returns.[4] When the indexes or the sensitivities are prespecified, generally a natural scaling occurs and a set of indexes suggests itself. When a researcher uses techniques that produce a model that best captures the past return structure, he or she must realize that the resulting structure is not unique. Some researchers will examine alternative structures in an attempt to under-

---

[3] Principal components analysis does provide one particular determinate solution to the factor solution. See the appendix to this paper.

[4] In technical terms, solutions are determined only up to a linear transformation of the factor structure.

stand what influences are affecting security returns and to convince themselves that the overall separation makes intuitive sense.

Nonuniqueness is a concern in certain applications and not in others. Any solution is correct in the sense that it explains (and predicts) returns as well as any other solution. Some solutions, however, are easier to interpret economically than others. Also, two researchers using slightly different solution algorithms or slightly different samples can come up with solutions that are simply transformations of each other but that appear to be very different.

Computational Problems.   A fourth problem with factor analysis is the difficulty of factor analyzing returns for a large number of securities. The primary problem is computational. Analyzing a large number of securities is costly and impossible to do with most standard statistical packages. To get a meaningful factor analysis, however, requires a longer data series than the number of firms being analyzed. With 20 years of monthly data, one is restricted to fewer than 240 firms.

Two procedures have been introduced to deal with difficulties in factor analyzing a large number of securities. The first involves performing factor analysis on subsets or groups of securities. This multisample approach was introduced by Roll and Ross (1980). The second is the portfolio approach introduced by Chen (1983).

In the group, or multisample, approach, securities are divided into samples and maximum likelihood factor analysis is used to extract factors from each sample.[5] The difficulty with this approach is that, because of indeterminacy, the factors extracted in each sample need not be extracted in the same order or even with the same sign. How then can one determine whether the same factors or different factors (unique to each group) have been extracted in going from group to group? The solution to this problem represents an opportunity to improve our identification of the return-generating process. By analyzing the factors produced from different groups and identifying those influences that are common across two or more groups, we can differentiate between factors unique to one group and general factors that apply to all groups.

Chen's approach rests on examining the return behavior of portfolios of securities rather than individual issues. This approach has two disadvantages. First, no matter how large the sample used to form portfolios, one cannot tell whether the factors are unique to that sample or common to all securities.

---

[5] Two papers, Cho, Elton, and Gruber (1984) and Brown and Weinstein (1983), discuss techniques for identifying the common factors across groups.

Second, the results obtained by this methodology are very sensitive to the portfolio formation technique that was used.

Applications of Multi-Index Models

In this section, we will discuss one simple example to illustrate the principles discussed earlier, and then we will describe two applications: one to the Japanese equity market and the second to the U.S. bond market. The purposes of these examples are to illustrate the basic ideas discussed earlier and to convey to the reader the kinds of tests and verification that are needed to be confident that the models are useful.

A Simple Example. To illustrate the principles discussed earlier, we ran a principal components analysis on historical return data for four market indexes. The indexes were the Morgan Stanley Capital International return indexes for common stocks in Canada, the United States, France, and Belgium. The data were monthly return data for the decade ending December 1988. The Morgan Stanley indexes are market-weighted indexes of the major stocks in each market. Table 1 shows the variance–covariance matrix and the correlation matrix. The variance entries are on the diagonal of the matrix, the covariance entries are above the diagonal, and the correlations are below the diagonal. The returns are positively correlated between all pairs of countries, and the highest correlation is between the two North American countries and the two European countries. Thus, two indexes will be needed: a general world index and an index that reflects whether the country is North American or European.

TABLE 1. Variance–Covariance Matrix and Correlations

Country	Belgium	Canada	France	United States
Belgium	50.34	17.55	34.22	13.79
Canada	0.38	42.41	19.64	22.39
France	0.65	0.41	55.11	15.64
United States	0.41	0.72	0.43	23.03

We ran a principal components analysis on the variance–covariance matrix and obtained two explanatory factors. The return on one factor was given by

$$f_{1t} = 0.67(R_{Bt} - \bar{R}_B) + 0.76(R_{Ct} - \bar{R}_C) + 0.76(R_{Ft} - \bar{R}_F)$$

$$+ 0.77(R_{Ut} - \bar{R}_U), \tag{3}$$

where

R = return,
f = factor value,
B = Belgium,
C = Canada,
U = United States,
F = France, and
t = time period.

Note from equation (3) that the first index is very close to an equally weighted index of the four country indexes. Thus, we might label the first factor a "world" factor.

The second factor is

$$f_{2,t} = -0.40(R_{Bt} - \bar{R}_B) + 0.73(R_{Ct} - \bar{R}_C) - 0.37(R_{Ft} - \bar{R}_F)$$
$$+ 0.41(R_{Ut} - \bar{R}_U). \tag{4}$$

This index is long in North America and short in Europe. It could be characterized as measuring the performance of North American stocks relative to Europe. The returns for each country and on each of the two factors for the last four months of our sample period are shown in Table 2.

TABLE 2. Returns in Countries and on Factors

Period	Belgium	Canada	France	U.S.	Index 1	Index 2
1	2.08%	14.64%	7.25%	6.08%	10.99%	9.85%
2	−4.95	13.41	−0.89	−1.03	−0.84	11.83
3	−16.57	−22.03	−15.95	−8.82	−34.85	−7.16
4	18.72	3.36	11.00	4.33	17.24	−7.13
Mean for 120 months	2.16	1.02	1.54	1.33		

Note: To get the return on the index, subtract the mean return shown at the bottom of the table from each month's return.

The b's (the sensitivities, or factor loadings) could be estimated by regressing the country returns on the two factors. Alternatively, the sensitivities are an output of the analysis. As one would expect, the b's are positive for the North American countries and negative for the European countries on the second index. The R^2s (explanatory power) of the two-index model for each country were 0.81 for Belgium, 0.95 for Canada, 0.84 for France, and 0.74 for the United States. The two-factor model does an excellent job of explaining returns.

A Multi-Index Model of the Japanese Stock Market. We selected Japanese data to demonstrate factor analytical solutions because of general interest in the Japanese markets and because Japan is an economy for which the multi-index models have an especially clear-cut advantage over the single-index model.[6] The sample of stocks originally selected for study was the 400 stocks that make up the Nomura Research Institute (NRI) 400 stock index. The Nomura Index, like the S&P Index, is market weighted. The 400 stocks in the index are among the largest in Japan, and attention is given to industry balance in selecting them. The 400 stocks in this index represent more than 60 percent of the total market value of all stocks listed on the Tokyo stock exchange. Seven of the stocks had incomplete data and were dropped from our sample.

We divided the remaining 393 securities into four approximately equal-sized samples. We then performed maximum likelihood factor analysis on the variance–covariance matrixes for each of these groups. The input data were the returns for each security for 180 months.

How many factors? The first problem in doing a factor analysis is deciding on the appropriate number of factors to include in the model. Tests of the appropriate number of factors can be separated into those that look at one group at a time and those that take advantage of the fact that solutions for more than one group have been obtained. Although we will emphasize the latter because it focuses on the commonality of the factors across groups, we will briefly examine the standard single-group tests.

Single-group tests. To obtain an initial idea of how many factors might be present in the return-generating process, ten factor solutions (using maximum likelihood factor analysis) were performed on each of our four samples. That is, for each sample, a maximum likelihood solution involving first one factor, then two factors, then three factors, and continuing through ten factors was calculated. Three techniques in the literature on factor analysis are commonly used to decide on the correct number of factors needed to explain the covariance matrix. These are chi square (Lawley & Maxwell 1971), information

---

[6] This section is based on an article by Elton and Gruber (1990). Other authors have documented the success of alternative forms of multi-index models in Japan. See Brown (1990) and Hamao (1990). The reason the multi-index model works especially well in Japan is the higher residual covariance between security returns after the influence of the market has been removed. This result may be attributable to some structural difference between the U.S. and Japanese economies or it may be attributable to the high percentage of corporate cross-ownership in Japan.

criteria (Akaike 1974b), and Baysian criteria (Schwartz 1978). Of the three, Schwartz's technique is the most conservative in estimating the number of significant factors. The chi square test and Akaike's information criteria tend to include factors that, although statistically significant, have little economic importance. When we used either of those two tests, the results showed that, for each sample, at least ten factors were present in the return-generating process. We did not test for the optimum number because we had not performed factor solutions involving the extraction of more than ten factors. Also, alternative tests, as well as previous attempts by others to identify the return-generation processes for other samples of securities, indicated the presence of fewer than ten factors.[7]

Schwartz's Baysian criteria provided a much more parsimonious description of the return-generating process. Schwartz's method produces a statistic that reaches its minimum at the "correct" number of factors extracted. The value of Schwartz's statistic for each group for alternative numbers of factors (one through ten) is shown in Figure 1. Schwartz's criteria identified three factors as significant in the return-generating process for Sample 1 and four factors for Samples 2, 3, and 4.

The conclusion from examining the number of factors present in the return-generating process of each sample separately is somewhat ambiguous. It rests on the choice of the test used to determine significance. The answer would seem to be either four, ten, or more factors. This ambiguity illustrates how cautious one should be about placing too much reliance on statistical significance in deciding on the number of factors. The next step is to use information from more than one group to decide on the number of factors.

Multiple-group tests. The intent of our analysis was to estimate a return-generating process that describes the return on all stocks that are comparable to the stocks in the NRI 400 Index. For any one of the four samples, as more factors were added to the solution, the probability increased that the added factors are idiosyncratic to the stocks in that sample or a subset of those stocks rather than factors that explain the covariance structure of returns among large groups of securities. If, in fact, the factor solution from a sample captured general influences, then the solution from a second group should reflect the same general influences. We could not, however, simply compare the first factor from a sample with the first factor from another sample and the second with the second, and so forth. Factor solutions are only unique up to a linear transformation. Therefore, the first factor from one sample may be the second

---

[7] See, for example, Roll and Ross (1980), Hamao (1990).

FIGURE 1.   Schwartz's Baysian Criterion

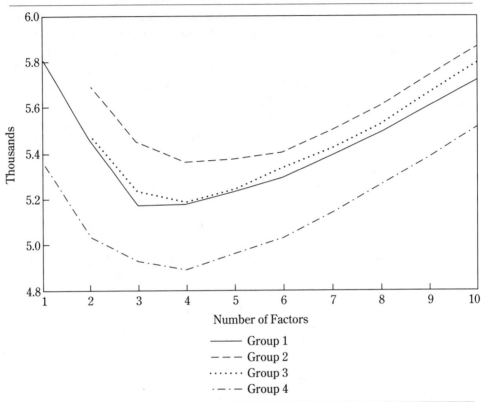

factor from a second sample or even a linear combination of the first, second, third, and fourth factors from the second sample. Although some attributes of maximum likelihood factor analysis will tend to extract factors in a parallel manner and to some extent lessen this problem, they do not eliminate it.[8]

This problem can be corrected by canonical correlation. For an n-factor solution, find that linear combination of the n factors from one sample that is most highly correlated with the best linear combination of the n factors from a second sample. After removing this correlation, find the second linear combination of the n factors from the first sample that is most highly correlated with the linear combination of the n factors from the second sample. This process is repeated n times. By finding best-fit linear combinations, canonical correlation removes the problem of factors from one sample being linear transformations of

---

[8] See Roll and Ross (1980) and Dhrymes et al. (1984) for a debate on this issue.

factors from a second sample. If, in fact, one has estimated too many factors, then after removing the common factors, the remaining canonical variates should be uncorrelated.

Table 3 presents the average (across four samples) squared canonical correlation for the first canonical variate out of the one-factor solution, the second canonical variate out of the two-factor solution, proceeding through the seventh canonical variate out of the seven-factor solution. The results indicate that the likely solution is either four or five factors. The canonical R^2 of the fourth linear combination from a four-factor solution is almost 60 percent; for the fifth linear combination from a five-factor solution, it is slightly more than 20 percent; but for the sixth linear combination of the six-factor solution, it is less than 5 percent.

TABLE 3. Canonical R, ith Canonical R^2 from the i Factor Solution

i	R^2
1	0.929
2	0.799
3	0.664
4	0.589
5	0.211
6	0.043
7	0.028

The evidence so far would seem to support a four-factor solution with the fifth factor worth considering. Although we have argued that canonical correlation is the correct way to determine whether factor structures from one group are the same as those from a second group, the simple correlation pattern between factors is also worth examining in order to see the type of orthogonal transformation that can take place. Table 4 presents the simple correlation between the factors extracted from Samples 1 and 2 for the four-factor and five-factor solutions. Note that in the four-factor solution, the only correlations above 0.10 occur for the first factor from Sample 1 with the first factor from Sample 2, the second with the second, and so forth. For the five-factor solution, however, this clear pattern fractures. In addition, some factors from one group do not seem to be associated at all with factors from the other group. For example, Factor 5 from Sample 1 and Factor 4 from Sample 2 have only minimal correlation with any of the factors from the other group. This result also supports the four-factor solution.

TABLE 4. An Example of a Factor Pattern: Correlation of Factor between Samples 1 and 2

	Sample 1				
Sample 2	F1	F2	F3	F4	F5
Four factors					
F1	0.974	—	—	—	
F2	—	0.895	—	—	
F3	—	—	0.904	—	
F4	—	—	—	0.690	
Five factors					
F1	0.973	—	—	—	—
F2	—	0.863	—	0.220	—
F3	—	—	0.901	—	—
F4	—	—	—	—	0.721
F5	—	0.174	−0.185	—	—

Note: Dash = less than 0.1.

With one four-factor solution for each of the four groups, the problem could be which solution to accept, but this is not really a problem. Each four-factor solution is close to a linear transformation of any other four-factor solution. Therefore, they should, for all practical purposes, work about equally well in explaining returns. In fact, they all have about the same explanatory power across securities and portfolios of securities. For example, the R^2 of the Tokyo Stock Exchange (TSE) varied between 0.902 to 0.928 across the four different factor solutions.

The model's explanatory power. Having determined that returns are related to four factors and having produced a particular four-factor solution, the next step is to examine how much of the total return these four factors explain and to compare this result to the amount explained by the more conventional single-index model.

To examine this question, we used returns on 20 groups obtained by ranking the securities in the NRI 400 by size (total equity asset capitalization). Grouping by size will, of course, increase the amount explained by almost any model. At the same time, it creates a manageable set of data that allows examination of average explanatory power and explanatory power across sets of stocks.

Table 5 shows the sensitivities and adjusted R^2s when the returns on each of the 20 portfolios are regressed against the four factors for the 15-year period April 1971 to March 1986. Across the 20 portfolios, the average adjusted R^2 is 78 percent. Of the 80 different sensitivity estimates, all but 18 are significant at the 5 percent level.

TABLE 5. Sensitivities and Explanatory Power for the Four-Factor Model

Portfolio	Beta Coefficients				Adjusted R^2
	F1	F2	F3	F4	
1	0.0428	0.0092	−0.0088	−0.0199	0.8168
2	0.0442	0.0048	−0.0048	−0.0203	0.8201
3	0.0427	0.0034	−0.0067	−0.0158	0.8580
4	0.0417	−0.0003[a]	−0.0060	−0.0137	0.8239
5	0.0421	0.0041	−0.0001[a]	−0.0121	0.7516
6	0.0396	0.0022[a]	−0.0030[a]	−0.0066	0.7689
7	0.0388	0.0077	0.0034[a]	−0.0028[a]	0.7504
8	0.0380	0.0078	0.0013[a]	0.0013[a]	0.7767
9	0.0417	0.0059	0.0011[a]	0.0010[a]	0.8130
10	0.0356	0.0025[a]	0.0020[a]	0.0001[a]	0.7266
11	0.0375	0.0023[a]	0.0071	0.0051	0.7732
12	0.0384	−0.0007[a]	0.0101	0.0053	0.7642
13	0.0347	−0.0037	0.0104	0.0084	0.7479
14	0.0374	−0.0029[a]	0.0084	0.0134	0.8112
15	0.0368	−0.0037	0.0100	0.0138	0.7605
16	0.0384	−0.0059	0.0118	0.0168	0.8086
17	0.0330	−0.0087	0.0134	0.0179	0.7395
18	0.0385	−0.0004[a]	0.0152	0.0151	0.7371
19	0.0364	−0.0022[a]	0.0163	0.0194	0.6995
20	0.0364	−0.0065	0.0171	0.0230	0.6626
Average					0.7755

[a]Insignificant at the 5 percent level.

To compare these results with those for the single-index model, returns on the 20 portfolios were regressed against the NRI 400 index. Because the NRI 400 index is value weighted and because it is made up of the same 400 stocks used to form the 20 groups, the relationship between the 20 portfolios and the index is likely to be higher than if we had chosen another market index. Table 6 shows the results. As one might expect given the construction of the index,

TABLE 6. Sensitivity and Explanatory Power for One-Index Model

Portfolio	Beta Coefficient	Adjusted R^2	Alpha	Average Return
1	1.1373	0.9065	−0.0018	0.0117
2	1.1289	0.8790	−0.0030	0.0104
3	1.0283	0.8700	0.0000	0.0122
4	0.9610	0.8180	−0.0002	0.0112
5	0.9570	0.7649	0.0030	0.0144
6	0.8697	0.7525	0.0007	0.0110
7	0.7877	0.6675	0.0022	0.0115
8	0.7942	0.6693	0.0038	0.0132
9	0.8130	0.6904	0.0000	0.0096
10	0.7067	0.5650	0.0069	0.0153
11	0.7037	0.5610	0.0037	0.0121
12	0.7097	0.5081	0.0036	0.0120
13	0.6232	0.4174	0.0098	0.0172
14	0.6203	0.4022	0.0058	0.0132
15	0.6307	0.3663	0.0073	0.0147
16	0.6137	0.3365	0.0106	0.0179
17	0.4815	0.2137	0.0124	0.0181
18	0.6001	0.2916	0.0109	0.0180
19	0.5349	0.2083	0.0135	0.0199
20	0.4841	0.1439	0.0203	0.0260
Average		0.5516		

the R^2 declines with size. The extent of the decline is dramatic. The adjusted R^2 is less than 50 percent for the smaller eight portfolios and less than 15 percent for the portfolio of smallest stocks. The four-factor model explains considerably more of the time series of security returns than does the single-factor model. The average adjusted R^2 is 55 percent compared with 78 percent for the four-factor model.[9]

Comparing the explanatory power of the first factor in the four-factor model with the explanatory power when all four factors are included shows that the added three factors explain a significant proportion of the variability of returns.

The sensitivity of portfolio returns to the NRI 400 index (beta) also declines

---

[9] That the four-factor model has a higher explanatory power than a single-factor market model in the fit period is to be expected. The size of the difference, however, is not the same as for U.S. studies, nor is the deterioration with size.

with size, which was not at all expected, because beta is usually considered a measure of risk. For U.S. data, the beta coefficient increases as size decreases, so smaller firms are viewed as having greater risk. For Japanese data, the reverse is true. This result must be interpreted with some caution, however. The firms in the sample are all fairly large. The 400 companies that compose the NRI 400 are selected from among the largest firms on the TSE, which lists 1,100 firms in its first section. Thus, the relationship between size and beta is found in the larger firms of the first section of the TSE.

Also evident from Table 6 is that return is strongly related to size. The difference between the average return on the small and large firms is more than 1 percent a month. Furthermore, the relationship is almost monotonic. These results mean that the smaller firms provide a higher return as well as lower beta. If beta is a risk measure, this evidence strongly favors the purchase of small stocks. Alternatively, perhaps beta is not a sufficient metric for risk. The relationship between return and size is at least partially captured by the four-factor model. For example, the sensitivities shown to Factor 4 are ranked by size. A similar pattern, although less pronounced, is seen in Factors 2 and 3. Thus, part of what the four-factor model is picking up relative to the one-factor model is a size effect.

Factor sensitivity stationarity. Another interesting question is the stability of the sensitivity coefficient, b_{ij}. We concentrated on Factor 4 because it generally has the least stable sensitivity of the four factors. Table 7 shows the sensitivity coefficients for Factor 4 for the 15-year period and three nonoverlapping 5-year periods. Although not identical, clearly the sensitivities have the same pattern across the 20 groups. The correlation between the sensitivities for the 1971–76 and 1976–81 periods is 0.97; the correlation between the 1976–81 and 1981–86 periods is 0.95.

The average absolute difference in sensitivity between the 1971–76 and 1976–81 periods was 0.0024 when the average absolute value of the sensitivity in the 1971–76 period was 0.0105. On average, the change was less than 23 percent. Likewise, the average absolute difference in sensitivity between the 1976–81 and 1981–86 periods was 0.0039, with an average absolute value of the sensitivity in 1976 to 1981 of 0.0139. Thus, the average change was about 28 percent. The sensitivity measures between nonoverlapping periods are very stable for Factor 4. The stability is even more pronounced for the other factors.

In this section, we have shown that a four-factor model explains returns better than a one-factor model and exhibits stable sensitivities over time. Although some increase in explanatory power is guaranteed as we move from a one-factor to a four-factor model, the magnitude of the increase, particularly for low-capitalization portfolios was unusually large. A much more powerful test

TABLE 7. Sensitivity to Factor 4

Portfolio	April 1976– March 1986	April 1981– March 1986	April 1976– March 1981	April 1971– March 1976
1	−0.0199	−0.0261	−0.0196	−0.0155
2	−0.0203	−0.0219	−0.0193	−0.0164
3	−0.0158	−0.0180	−0.0162	−0.0135
4	−0.0137	−0.0173	−0.0109	−0.0127
5	−0.0121	−0.0068[a]	−0.0107	−0.0162
6	−0.0066	−0.0018[a]	−0.0073	−0.0074
7	−0.0028[a]	0.0040[a]	−0.0048[a]	−0.0045[a]
8	0.0013[a]	0.0042[a]	−0.0009[a]	0.0031[a]
9	0.0010[a]	−0.0006[a]	0.0018[a]	0.0002[a]
10	0.0001[a]	0.0031[a]	0.0005[a]	−0.0008[a]
11	0.0051	0.0055[a]	0.0057[a]	0.0043[a]
12	0.0053	0.0073	0.0069	0.0037[a]
13	0.0084	0.0126	0.0049[a]	0.0060
14	0.0134	0.0084	0.0156	0.0140
15	0.0138	0.0180	0.0172	0.0083
16	0.0168	0.0125	0.0164	0.0177
17	0.0179	0.0187	0.0133	0.0155
18	0.0151	0.0133	0.0134	0.0132
19	0.0194	0.0230	0.0165	0.0153
20	0.0230	0.0238	0.0234	0.0216

[a]Insignificant at 5 percent level.

of whether a four-factor model is superior to the one-index model is to make comparisons in a forecast mode. We will now examine one such comparison.

Index Matching. In index matching, for each model (the one-index and four-index models), a portfolio is constructed that has the same sensitivity (beta) or sensitivities as the index being matched, with minimum residual risk and (approximately) a fixed number of securities. The second step is to examine the ability of these portfolios to match the index over a period of time subsequent to when they are formed.

The index-matching test is a joint test of a number of hypotheses. One aspect affecting performance is whether the market has one or four factors. Even with four factors, the one-factor model could still perform better than the four-factor model if the historically estimated sensitivities for the four-factor model were poor forecasts of future sensitivities and the historical sensitivities for the single-index model were a good predictor of future sensitivities. Finally, if the sensitivity of the market to the four factors is very stable over time, the performance of the two models might be quite similar, even if the four-factor model were a superior description of reality. In this case, matching market betas is equivalent to matching factor sensitivities. Thus, the index-matching tests are joint tests of the model, the stability of the sensitivities, and the stability of the relationship of the market to the factors.

We attempted to match the Nikkei 225 Index over the five-year period January 1, 1981, to December 31, 1986. The first step was estimating sensitivities for each security. Sensitivities were estimated on a quarterly basis for both the single-factor model and the four-factor model. For the market model, we simply ran a regression of the return on each of the 393 stocks in our study against the TSE Index at the beginning of each quarter using the previous five years of monthly data. For the four-factor model, a factor analysis was run at the beginning of each quarter, using the prior 11 years of return data to determine the composition of the factors. Then, at the beginning of each quarter, we regressed the prior five years of monthly returns for each of the 393 securities against returns on the four factors. The regression coefficients were the sensitivities or betas used in the next step. To match the Nikkei, we need to know the sensitivity of that index to our model. To estimate the sensitivity of the Nikkei 225, we regressed it against both the TSE Index for the market model and the four indexes for the four-factor model.

Once the sensitivities were determined, we calculated the composition of the portfolio with minimum tracking error. Matching portfolios were determined for portfolios of about 25, 50, and 100 securities. For example, for the market model with 25 securities, quadratic programming was used to produce a portfolio with approximately 25 securities that (1) had the same beta as the Nikkei index and minimal residual risk from the market model, (2) involved full investment, and (3) had appropriate upper and lower limits on investment in each security.[10] For the four-factor model, the portfolio is constrained to match the sensitivity of the Nikkei index to each of the four factors. This procedure is repeated for 25, 50, and 100 securities and for each quarter, or 20 times for the five-year period.

Having determined the portfolio composition at the beginning of each quarter, we then calculated the return on the Nikkei 225 adjusted for dividends each month, as well as the return on the matching portfolio, using the market

[10] Getting the quadratic programming solution to contain approximately 25 securities involved iterating the solution for different limits on the fraction invested in each security.

model and the matching portfolio for the four-factor model.[11] To determine which model matched the adjusted Nikkei 225 more closely, we calculated the monthly difference in return between the index and the matching portfolio and squared it. We then computed the average squared difference between the index and the two matching portfolios expressed as a percentage of return. Because financial stocks are thinly traded, in a further test, they were excluded from the matching portfolio. This test was to examine the ability to match when a segment of the market is excluded.

Figure 2 presents results for portfolios of 25, 50, and 100 stocks and for the 50-stock nonfinancial portfolio. In all four tests, the matching portfolios formed using four factors outperformed the matching portfolios using one factor. The

FIGURE 2. Difference in Return of Single- and Four-Factor Models

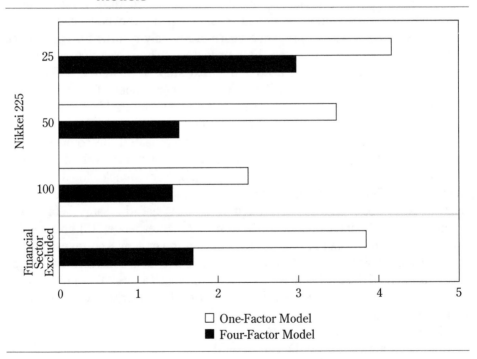

[11] Dividends averaged about 1 percent a year. Dividend payments were implicitly reinvested in the portfolio at the proportions existing at the time the stock went ex-dividend.

four-factor model cut the average squared forecasting error, in some cases, by more than half.

The index-matching test involves forecasting the model and parameters. Thus, the difference in number of factors during the fit period does not bias the results. The ability of the four-factor model to allow the construction of a portfolio that tracks a second portfolio more closely is powerful evidence that the four-factor model describes reality better than the single-factor model.[12]

A Multi-Index Model of Bond Returns. As a second example of the estimation of a multi-index model from historical returns, we will discuss an application to bonds. In this case, we were attempting to find a return-generating model that would be useful in protecting against shifts in the term structure of interest rates.

Estimation of a multi-index model using bond returns has a basic problem. An assumption underlying most estimation techniques is that the structure of the multi-index model remains stable over time. For bond returns, however, this is unlikely to be true. The factor determining how bond returns move together is a shift in the term structure, which affects long bonds more than short. Further, examining the return series for a single bond would mean that the return series is for a bond with changing maturity and changing sensitivity to a shift in the term structure over time. To mitigate this influence, each of the portfolios of bonds for which a time series of returns was constructed had a constant maturity over time and hence roughly a constant sensitivity to the factors.

Using these time series, we constructed the correlation matrix by standardizing returns to have a mean of zero and a variance of 1. We used the correlation matrix because of evidence of Gibbons (1982) that factor analysis of the correlation matrix for U.S. bond data is more stable than factor analysis of the variance–covariance matrix. We then performed a maximum likelihood factor analysis on the correlation matrix. To obtain indexes over a large sample, we constructed portfolios of bonds that were perfectly correlated with each factor from the factor analysis and that were uncorrelated with other indexes. We then estimated the sensitivities by using least squares regression of the constant-maturity portfolios on the indexes.

The question now is how to decide if this multi-index model is useful. We

---

[12] As we discussed earlier, this is a joint test. It is not very plausible, however, that the four-factor model is more stable than the one-factor model. Its superior performance is likely to be because of the presence of multiple factors rather than greater stability of sensitivities.

examined its usefulness on a relative basis: Did it perform better than alternatives others had suggested? We compared this multi-index model with other models in which either the indexes or the sensitivities (durations) were prespecified. We examined both a single-index and a two-index model. We stopped at two indexes because, after removing two indexes, the covariance between unique return, $E(e_i e_j)$, for our portfolios was so close to zero that extracting additional indexes was not feasible.

We used three different sets of tests.[13] First, we examined which model serves as a better forecaster of future returns. Within the period that the factors are extracted, the two-index model would explain more than the one index. If the second index is spurious, however, or if sensitivity to the second index is unstable over time, then the single-index model might well work best. The models were compared by examining the average absolute difference between forecasted return and actual return.

The second tests were correlation tests. If a multi-index model is the correct one, then the covariance of unique return across portfolios, $E(e_i e_j)$, should be close to zero. Once again, this idea was tested for forecasted returns. In this case, we compared the average absolute value of the covariance between residuals.

The third test has its origins in immunization. The cash flows from an arbitrary portfolio of bonds was used to represent a set of liabilities. Because the value of the portfolio of liabilities at each point is known, the change in value of the liabilities (the portfolio's return) can be calculated. We tried to immunize these liabilities by constructing a second portfolio of bonds that moved in unison with (had the same return as) the portfolio of liabilities. If we have the correct return-generating process, then a portfolio of assets with the same sensitivities to the factors as the liabilities should be immunized and differences in return should be random.

In this study, the two-index model outperformed the single-index models; for bonds, two factors seemed to be necessary. Furthermore, prespecifying the sensitivities as durations rather than estimating them from the data produced the poorest results. In this case, however, prespecifying the two indexes as returns on a widely diversified portfolio of short bonds and a widely diversified portfolio of long bonds outperformed the model for which the two indexes were estimated empirically by factor analysis. The factor structure was sufficiently unstable over time that it was better to select two portfolios widely separated

---

[13] See Elton, Gruber, and Nabar (1988) for a more detailed description of the methodology and results described in this section.

in maturity and broadly diversified and use them as the portfolios (indexes) of interest over time.

Conclusions

In this paper, we have reviewed some methodology for simultaneously estimating the indexes and sensitivities in a multi-index model. We have discussed some of the problems with this methodology and described one example, the Japanese stock market, for which the method worked extremely well, and one example, U.S. bonds, for which it worked less well.

We also described some tests of how well a factor model works. Two points are particularly important: Whether a model works well or poorly can only be judged in the framework of a particular application (and then it should be judged in a forecast mode), and the performance of the model is only good or bad relative to alternative models. Good performance is not an absolute concept.

We should close with a brief discussion of the methodology we have discussed in this chapter versus the methodology of prespecifying sensitivities or indexes. Estimating both parameters of a multi-index model has a characteristic that is both its fundamental strength and its major weakness. Its strength is that it requires no a priori specification of the influences that affect returns. This makes such models an ideal tool for explaining new types of data. This analysis can provide real insight into the influences that affect returns. Furthermore, an n-index model derived from a set of data via factor analysis explains those data better than any other n-index model. The weakness of the factor solution is that it may or may not perform better in any application involving forecasts. Moreover, the factor solution lacks the intuition contained in a model constructed on the basis of economic logic, and it is usually more difficult to explain to clients.

A researcher might well wish to use combinations of the models discussed in the various sections of this monograph. If an analyst feels confident that he or she can identify one or more economic variables that affect security returns but that other, unknown factors might be important, factor analysis can help identify these unknown factors. For example, a researcher might believe that all equity returns are affected by the market but that undefined sector influences are also instrumental. One solution is to estimate the single-index model using the market index and then factor analyze the residuals of the single-index model to derive other factors.

Appendix A

Several statistical techniques can be used to produce a set of indexes that explain the interrelationship among security returns. The most commonly used techniques for identifying the influences (factors) affecting security returns and sensitivities (factor loadings) simultaneously are principal component analysis and factor analysis.

Principal Component Analysis

Principal component analysis is perhaps easier to understand than factor analysis. For returns on a defined set of stocks over a predetermined time span, compute an index (weighted average of that set of returns) that explains the maximum amount of the variation in the variance–covariance matrix of security returns.[14] Usually, the first principal component looks somewhat like a market index with all stocks entering with positive weights. Then, search for the index, constrained to be orthogonal (uncorrelated with the first index), that explains as much as possible of the unexplained portion of the variance–covariance matrix. Additional principal components are then extracted until the user decides that they are picking up random influences in the data rather than real information. Of course, a prior estimate of the number of relevant influences will narrow the choice of how many principal components to extract.

To obtain a multi-index model from a principal component solution some adjustments are usually performed. First, the indexes obtained from a principal components solution have decreasing standard deviations as additional influ-

---

[14] Many researchers choose to perform principal component or factor analysis on the correlation matrix rather than the variance–covariance matrix. This choice is made because the solution is sensitive to the scale of the data. Although historical returns on securities have a natural scaling, an analyst may not want the solution to be affected by the difference in volatility across securities.

ences are extracted. Normally, the indexes are adjusted so the standard deviations of all indexes are unity.[15]

As additional influences are extracted using principal components analysis, the proportion of random noise in the yet-unexplained variance–covariance matrix increases. Therefore, each successive principal component is more likely to be measuring random influences.

Principal component analysis has several advantages over other methods of extracting factors:

- There is a unique solution.
- The meaning of successive factors is easy to understand.
- The solution technique is simple compared with most other factor solution techniques, and a large sample can be used.
- When residual variance across securities is unrelated to factor loadings and sample size goes to infinity, the principal component solution is a transformation of the factor solution while being solvable (see Connor and Korayczk 1986).

The major weakness of principal component analysis is that it is variance oriented rather than covariance oriented. The assumption is that residual variance is not related to factor loadings.[16]

Factor Analysis

Factor analysis operates directly on the covariance matrix and produces a result that is intuitively appealing, given the nature of multifactor models. A number of alternative estimation procedures are available, including maximum likelihood, generalized least squares, and unweighted least squares. Most analysts use maximum likelihood methods. For any hypothesized number of factors, factor analysis finds the indexes and the loadings on each index for each security to make the covariance between the unique returns as small as possible.

Although the indexes produced by factor analysis need not be orthogonal to

---

[15] In addition, researchers often want to construct the indexes from a larger sample of stocks or to have other properties such as being widely diversified. See, for example, Lehmann and Modest (1988).

[16] For example, in a single-index model, beta has been shown to be positively related to residual variance. Thus, a principal components estimation of the single-index model can lead to false inferences about beta.

each other, researchers in this area have generally constructed their solutions so that they are orthogonal. Even with the orthogonal constraint, interpreting the solution is quite complex. For any given data set, an infinite number of equivalent factor solutions are possible, which makes interpreting any particular factor very difficult. The information spanned by the multiple-factor solution from one sample should be the same as the information spanned by the multiple-factor solution from the second sample (except for sampling error). As a practical matter, we know what the set of factors from a factor solution represents, but we are less sure about the meaning of any individual factor.

A second drawback to factor analysis is that factor solutions are very difficult to estimate and the sample size that can be factor analyzed is limited by the length of the return series. Maximum likelihood factor analysis involves a complex nonlinear optimization problem. It is sufficiently complex that many analysts have resorted to small sample sizes to estimate factors and factor loadings.

Multiple-Factor Models for Portfolio Risk

Richard Grinold
Ronald N. Kahn
BARRA

Multiple-factor models have been applied to forecasting expected returns, as well as forecasting risk. This paper will focus on the use of multiple-factor models to predict and control portfolio risk rather than on their use to identify sources of expected return. Portfolio risk depends both on asset risks and on correlations; factor models accurately capture both of these characteristics. The goals of risk-forecasting models are to help portfolio managers analyze the sources of risk in their portfolios; to determine (*ex post*) if the risks were justified; and, with a forecast of expected returns, to build new portfolios that have desirable characteristics.

The emphasis in this paper is on factor models that are relatively easy for skilled investment practitioners to interpret and use. Thus, we will stress the use of factors that capture familiar investment themes such as value, growth, momentum, volatility, and size. We will also stress the use of models that quickly adapt to the changing nature of the marketplace, whether the change is the merger of U.S. Steel and Marathon Oil, the birth of the Baby Bells, the emergence of an electrical utilities industry in the United Kingdom, or a drastic reassessment of the earnings prospects for IBM.

A Brief History of Multiple-Factor Models

Modern portfolio theory started in the 1950s with Markowitz's (1959) statement of the portfolio management problem as one of balancing risk against expected return. He also stressed the role of diversification in reducing portfolio risk. In the 1960s, Lintner (1965a, 1965b), Mossin (1966), Sharpe (1964), and Treynor (1961) went one step further and proposed a single-factor model for the explanation of expected return. In the 1970s, Merton (1972), Rosenberg and Marathe (1975), Ross (1976), Sharpe (1977), and others proposed multiple-factor models for the explanation of expected returns. In the 1980s, academic debate still centered around the issue of expected return—in particular, the correct way to explain expected return on financial assets (asset pricing). The question was whether current statistical procedures are up to the task of recognizing the correct answer if we have it in hand.

Rosenberg (1974) noted early on that the same procedures used in the search for expected returns could also be used to explain portfolio risk. Moreover, these efforts had the benefits of being independent of any particular theory of expected returns and having practical value. They helped portfolio managers deal in a quantitative and effective way with the issue of risk control. With the help of a model to handle risk, the managers could then concentrate their efforts on the difficult task of finding assets that are potential over- or underachievers.

Multiple-factor risk models of equity returns are mentioned in a host of academic papers. They are usually not the focus of the paper, merely a technique or an abstract structure made to demonstrate the point. The literature on arbitrage pricing theory has made the multiple-factor model a standard part of the academic landscape. As is well known, the arbitrage pricing theory posits the existence of an unknown number of unidentified factors that can be used to explain expected returns. This vague specification has caused some scoffing, but it has also opened the door to a tremendous amount of creativity in building linear models. The rule seems to be "anything that is not forbidden is allowed." Given the wide availability of data, the low cost of computation, the human imagination, and the need to publish, attempts to build such models have taken widely different approaches. Witness, for example, the efforts of Roll and Ross (1980), Chen, Roll, and Ross (1986), Conner and Korajczyk (1988), and Lehmann and Modest (1988).

The Structure of Multiple-Factor Risk Models

The multiple-factor risk models described in this paper have a simple linear structure composed of four components: a stock's exposures to the factors, its excess returns, the attributed factor returns, and the specific returns. Formally,

$$r_n(t) = \sum_k X_{n,k}(t)f_k(t) + u_n(t), \tag{1}$$

where

$X_{n,k}(t)$ = the exposure of asset n to factor k (known at time t),
$r_n(t)$ = the excess return (return above the risk-free return) on stock n during the period from time t to time $t + 1$,
$f_k(t)$ = the factor return to factor k during the period from time t to time $t + 1$, and
$u_n(t)$ = stock n's specific return during the period from time t to time $t + 1$.[1] This is the return that cannot be explained by the factors.

The exposures, $X_{n,k}$, are frequently called *factor loadings*. For industry factors, the exposures are either 1 or 0, indicating whether or not the stock belongs to a given industry. For the other common factors, the exposures are standardized so that the average exposure over all stocks is 0 and the standard deviation across stocks is 1.

The specific return, u_n, is sometimes called the *idiosyncratic return* to the stock. It is the return the model does not explain. The risk model will account for specific risk, however, so the risk predictions will explicitly consider the risk of u_n.

Equation (1) is not meant to convey any sense of causality. The factors may or may not be the basic driving forces for security returns. In our view, they are merely dimensions along which to analyze risk.

Now, assume that the specific returns are not correlated with the factor returns and the specific returns are not correlated with each other. With these assumptions and the return structure of equation (1), the risk structure is:

$$V_{n,m} = \sum_{k1,k2=1}^{K} X_{n,k1}F_{k1,k2}X_{m,k2} + \Delta_{n,m}, \tag{2}$$

where

$V_{n,m}$ = the covariance of asset n with asset m *(if $n = m$, this gives the variance of asset n)*,
$X_{n,k1}$ = the exposure of asset n to factor $k1$,

---

[1] Although the model's time structure is defined in equation (1), in the rest of this paper, the explicit time variables will be suppressed.

$F_{k1,k2}$ = the covariance of factor $k1$ with factor $k2$ (if $k1 = k2$, this gives the variance of factor $k1$), and

$\Delta_{n,m}$ = the specific covariance of asset n with asset m. By assumption, all specific risk correlations are zero, so this term is zero unless $n = m$. In that case, this term gives the specific variance of asset n.

Building the Model

The process of building a multiple-factor risk model consists of three phases: choosing the factors, estimating factor returns, and forecasting risk. We shall examine these in detail.

Choosing the Factors. The art of building a multiple-factor risk model is to choose appropriate factors. This search for factors is limited by one key constraint: All factors must be a priori factors. That is, even though the factor returns are uncertain, the factor exposures must be known at the beginning of the period.

Within the constraint of a priori factors, a wide variety of factors are possible. To classify the factors, they are first divided into three categories: responses to external influences, cross-sectional comparisons of asset attributes, and purely internal or statistical factors.

• *Responses to external influences.* One of the prevalent themes in the academic literature of financial economics is that a demonstrable link should exist between outside economic forces and the equity markets. The response factors are an attempt to capture that link. These factors include responses to return in the bond market (sometimes called bond beta), unexpected changes in inflation (inflation surprise), changes in oil prices, changes in exchange rates, and changes in industrial production. These factors are sometimes called macrofactors. BARRA models use this type of factor, in particular in response to interest rate changes and, in some countries, response to changes in exchange rates.

These measures suffer from two serious defects. The first is that the response coefficient has to be estimated through regression analysis or some similar technique. This requirement leads to errors in the estimates, commonly called the error-in-variables problem. The second drawback is that the estimates are based on behavior during a past period, generally five years. Even if these past estimates are accurate in the statistical sense of capturing the true situation in the past, they may not accurately describe the present. In short, these response coefficients can be nonstationary.

• *Cross-sectional comparisons.* These factors, which have no link to the remainder of the economy, compare attributes of the stocks. Cross-sectional attributes can themselves be classified in two groups: fundamental and market. Fundamental attributes include such ratios as dividend yield and earnings yield, plus analysts' forecasts of future earnings per share. Market attributes include volatility during a past period, return during a past period, option-implied volatility, share turnover, and so forth.

To some extent, market attributes such as volatility and momentum may have the same difficulties (errors in variables, nonstationarity) as the external response factors. Here, however, the factor interpretation is somewhat different. For example, a momentum factor, taken to be a measure of the price performance of the stock for the past 12 months, is not intended as a forecast of continued success or of mean reversion. It is merely a recognition that stocks that have been relatively successful (unsuccessful) during the past year will quite frequently behave in a common fashion. Sometimes the momentum will be reinforced, in other times it will be reversed, and in yet other times it will be irrelevant. We are accounting for the fact that in five or six months of the year, controlling for other attributes, previously successful stocks behave in a much different manner than previously unsuccessful stocks. The same is true for stocks with high historical volatility and so forth.

- *Statistical factors*. It is possible to amass returns data on a large number of stocks, turn the crank of a statistical meat grinder, and admire the factors the machine produces: *factor ex machina*. This procedure can be accomplished in an amazingly large number of ways, including principal component analysis, maximum likelihood analysis, and expectations maximization analysis. One can use a two-step approach—first get the factors and then the exposures—or simultaneously estimate both factors and exposures, or turn the problem on its head in the imaginative approach taken by Connor and Korajczyk (1988). BARRA models do not usually include statistical factors because they are very difficult to interpret and because the statistical estimation procedure is prone to discovering spurious correlations.

Among the many possible factors, those chosen should satisfy three criteria: They should be incisive, intuitive, and interesting. *Incisive factors* differentiate returns. For example, low-volatility stocks perform differently from high-volatility stocks at least three times a year. If the overall volatility exposure is not monitored, then returns can be upset with disturbing frequency.

Intuitive factors relate to interpretable and recognizable dimensions of the market. Credible stories define these factors. For example, size has the big companies at one end and the small companies at the other. Momentum has the firms that have performed well separated from the firms that have done relatively poorly. Intuitive factors arise from recognizable investment themes.

Factors in the U.S. equity market include industries, size, yield, value, success, volatility, growth, leverage, liquidity, foreign income, and labor sensitivity.

Interesting factors explain some part of performance. We can attribute a certain amount of return to each factor in each period. That factor might help explain exceptional return or beta or volatility. For example, large stocks did well over a particular period, or high-volatility stocks are high-beta stocks.

Research leading to the appropriate factors, then, depends both on statistical techniques and on investment intuition. Statistical techniques can identify the most incisive and interesting factors. Investment intuition can help identify intuitive factors. Factors can have statistical significance or investment significance or both. Model research must take both forms of significance into account.

Exposures. The factors typically chosen for use in a multiple-factor risk model fall into two broad categories: industries and risk indexes. Industry factors measure the differing behavior of stocks in different industries. Risk indexes measure the differing behavior of stocks across other, nonindustry dimensions.

- *Industry exposures.* Industry groupings partition stocks into nonoverlapping classes. Industry groupings should satisfy several criteria. They should represent a reasonable number of companies in each industry, have a reasonable fraction of capitalization in each industry, and be in reasonable accord with the conventions and mind-set of investors in that market.

Industry exposures are usually 1/0 variables, because stocks are either in an industry or they are not. The market itself has unit exposure in total to the industries. Because large corporations can do business in several industries, the industry factors must account for multiple industry memberships. For example, for March 1992, BARRA's USE2 model classifies General Electric as 39 percent producer goods, 28 percent aerospace, 23 percent consumer products, 5 percent miscellaneous finance, and 5 percent media.

- *Risk index exposures.* Industries are not the only sources of stock risk. Risk indexes measure the movements of stocks exposed to common investment themes. Risk indexes we have identified in the United States and other equity markets fall into these broad categories:

> *Volatility* distinguishes stocks by their volatility. Assets that rank high in this dimension have been and are expected to be more volatile than average.
> *Momentum* distinguishes stocks by recent performance.
> *Size* distinguishes large stocks from small stocks.
> *Liquidity* distinguishes stocks by how often their shares trade.
> *Growth* distinguishes stocks by past and anticipated earnings growth.

Value distinguishes stocks by their fundamentals, including ratios of earnings, dividends, cash flows, book value, and sales to price; is the stock cheap or expensive relative to fundamentals?

Earnings volatility distinguishes stocks by their earnings stability.

Financial leverage distinguishes firms by their debt-to-equity ratios and exposure to interest rate risk.

Any particular equity market can contain fewer or more risk indexes, depending on its own idiosyncrasies.

Each of the broad categories listed above can contain several specific measurements, or *descriptors*, of the category. For instance, volatility measures might include recent daily return volatility, option-implied volatility, recent price range, and beta. Although the descriptors are typically correlated, each captures one aspect of the risk index. We construct risk index exposures by weighting exposures of the descriptors within the risk index. The weights are chosen to maximize the model's explanatory power. Relying on several different descriptors can improve model robustness.

The various categories of descriptors and risk indexes involve different sets of natural units and ranges. To quantify them, all raw exposure data must be rescaled:

$$X_{\text{normalized}} = \frac{X_{\text{raw}} - \text{mean}\ (X_{\text{raw}})}{SD(X_{\text{raw}})}, \tag{3}$$

where mean (X_{raw}) is the raw exposure value mean and $SD(X_{\text{raw}})$ is the raw exposure value standard deviation across the universe of assets. The result is that each risk index exposure has a mean of zero and a standard deviation of 1. This standardization also facilitates the handling of outliers.

As an example of how this procedure works, BARRA's USE2 model assigns General Motors a size exposure of 1.30 for March 1992. Thus, on the size dimension, General Motors lies significantly above average. For the same date, the model assigns Apple Computers a size exposure of -0.26. On this dimension, Apple Computers lies somewhat below average.

Factor Returns. Given exposures to the industry and risk index factors, the next step is to estimate returns via multiple regressions. This procedure was developed in Fama–MacBeth (1973). The model is linear, and equation (1) has the form of a multiple regression. Stock excess returns are regressed against factor exposures, choosing factor returns that minimize the (possibly weighted) sum of squared specific returns. For the United States, we use a universe of 1,100 of the largest companies. The R^2 statistic, which measures the explanatory power of the model, tends to average between 30 percent and 40 percent for models of monthly equity returns with roughly 1,000 assets and 50 factors. Larger R^2 statistics tend to occur in months with larger market moves.

In this cross-sectional regression, which is performed every period, generally one month, the industry factors play the role of intercepts. The market as a whole has an exposure of 1 to the industries, and industry factor returns tend to pick up the market return. They are the more volatile factors in the model. The market has close to zero exposure to the risk indexes, and risk index factor returns pick up extra-market returns. They are the less volatile factors in the market.

To estimate factor returns efficiently, we run generalized least squares regressions, weighting each observed return by the inverse of its specific variance. In some models, we instead weight each observation by the square root of its market capitalization, which acts as a proxy for the inverse of its specific variance.[2]

Although these cross-sectional regressions can involve many variables (the USE2 model uses 68 factors), the models do not suffer from multicollinearity. Most of the factors are industries (55 out of 68 in USE2), which are orthogonal. In addition, tests of variance inflation factors, which measure the inflation in estimate errors attributable to multicollinearity, lie far below serious danger levels.

Factor Portfolios.   The regression approach to estimating factor returns leads to an insightful interpretation of the factors. Weighted regression gymnastics lead to the following matrix expression for the estimated factor returns:

$$f = (X^T W X)^{-1} (X^T W r), \tag{4}$$

where X is the exposure matrix, W is the diagonal matrix of regression weights, and r is the vector of excess returns. For each particular factor return, this calculation is simply a weighted sum of excess returns:

$$f_k = \sum_{n=1}^{N} C_{k,n} r_n. \tag{5}$$

---

[2] Our research has shown that the square root is the appropriate power of market capitalization to mimic inverse specific variance. Larger companies have lower specific variance, and as company size doubles, market variance shrinks by a factor of 0.7.

In this form, each factor return, f_k, can be interpreted as the return to a portfolio with portfolio weights $c_{k,n}$. So factor returns are the returns to *factor portfolios*. The factor portfolio holdings, which are known a priori, ensure that the portfolio has unit exposure to the particular factor, zero exposure to every other factor, and minimum risk, given those constraints.

These portfolios have two different interpretations. They are sometimes interpreted as *factor-mimicking portfolios*, because they mimic the behavior of some underlying basic factor. We interpret them more simply as portfolios that capture the specific effect we have defined through our exposures.

Factor portfolios typically contain both long and short positions. For example, the factor portfolio for the earnings-to-price factor in the U.S. market will have an earnings-to-price ratio that is one standard deviation above the market while having zero exposure to all other factors. A zero exposure to an industry implies that the portfolio will hold some industry stocks long and others short, with longs and shorts balancing. This portfolio will contain every single asset with some weight.

Factor Covariance and Specific-Risk Matrixes. Once the factor returns each period are estimated, we can estimate a factor covariance matrix—an estimate of all the factor variances and covariances. To operate effectively as a risk model, this factor covariance matrix should constitute our best forecast of future factor variances and covariances over the investor's time horizon.[3]

Generating an asset-by-asset covariance matrix requires both the factor covariance matrix, F, and the specific risk matrix, Δ. By definition, a stock's specific return, u_n, is that component of its return that the model cannot explain. So the multiple-factor model can provide no insight into stock-specific returns. For specific risk, we need to model specific return variance, u_n^2 assuming that mean specific return is zero.

In general, the model for specific risk is

$$u_n^2(t) = S(t)[1 + v_n(t)], \tag{6}$$

with

---

[3] Forecasting covariance from a past history of factor returns is a subject worthy of a paper in itself, and the details are beyond the scope of this effort. Basic techniques rely on weights over the past history and Bayesian priors on covariance. More advanced techniques include forecasting variance conditional on recent events, as first suggested by Engle (1982). Such techniques assume that variance is only constant conditional on other variables. For a review of these ideas, see Bollerslev et al. (1992).

$$\left(\frac{1}{N}\right)\sum_{n=1}^{N}u_n^2(t) = S(t) \tag{7}$$

and

$$\left(\frac{1}{N}\right)\sum_{n=1}^{N}v_n(t) = 0. \tag{8}$$

$S(t)$ measures the average specific variance across the universe of stocks, and v_n captures the cross-sectional variation in specific variance.

To forecast specific risk, we use a time series model for $S(t)$ and a linear multiple-factor model for $v_n(t)$. Models for $v_n(t)$ typically include some risk index factors, plus factors measuring recent squared specific returns. The time dependence in the model of $v_n(t)$ is captured by time variation in the exposures. One pooled regression over assets and time periods, with outliers trimmed, is used to estimate model coefficients.

Data Requirements.   Multiple-factor risk models require data on stock returns and sufficient data to calculate factor exposures. Calculating stock returns requires not only stock price data but also data on stock dividends, splits, and other adjustments. Factor exposures require industry identification, including earnings, sales, and assets segmented by industry; historical returns; associated option information; fundamental accounting data; and earnings forecasts.[4]

Model Validity

Considerable evidence supports the validity of multiple-factor risk models. This evidence falls into three categories: in-sample tests, out-of-sample tests, and empirical observations.

In-sample tests focus on the performance of the multiple-factor model (equation 1) in explaining excess stock returns. Typically, these models will use

---

[4] BARRA's USE2 model started in January 1973 and, for initial estimation, required data covering the period from January 1968 through December 1972. This model relies mainly on MARKET PLUS for market data, COMPUSTAT for fundamental accounting data, and IBES for earnings forecasts, but it also requires data from many other sources, including Standard & Poor's, the New York Stock Exchange, the American Stock Exchange, Value Line, and Interactive Data Corporation.

roughly 50 factors to explain the returns to roughly 1,000 assets each month. Monthly R^2 statistics for the models average about 30–40 percent, meaning that the model "explains," on average, about 30–40 percent of the observed cross-sectional variance of the universe of stock returns.

These R^2 statistics, averaged over many months, do not accurately convey model performance, however. In fact, the R^2 statistic can vary quite significantly from month to month, depending in part on the overall market return. Model R^2 statistics are highest when the market return differs very significantly from zero. The R^2 statistic was very high in October 1987 because the market return was so extreme. In months when the market return is near zero, the R^2 statistic can be quite low, even if discrepancies between realized and modeled returns are small.

Another measure of model performance is the root mean square error from the regression. This averages 6 percent for monthly cross-sectional returns in the United States and does not vary much from month to month. Because monthly stock volatility in the United States averages 10 percent, the model explains about 64 percent of individual stock variance, on average.

Because the goal of the model is to explain portfolio risk, a better way to evaluate the model is by the fraction of portfolio risk it explains, and here is evidence of the model's true power. For benchmark portfolios in the United States, the multiple-factor risk model explains more than 98 percent of portfolio variance.

Out-of-sample tests compare forecast risk with realized risk. One out-of-sample test builds portfolios of randomly chosen assets and then compares the forecast and realized active risk of those portfolios; active risk is defined as the volatility of the active return, or the difference between the portfolio return and a benchmark return. In tests in the United States involving 500 such portfolios containing 100 assets each, we compared realized active risk for a 12-month period with forecast active risk at the beginning of the 1988–91 period, using the S&P 500 as the benchmark. At the 1 percent confidence level, we could reject the hypothesis that forecast variance equaled realized variance only 2.8 percent of the time.

We have also examined risk forecasts cross-sectionally. With the same 500 portfolios, we examined standardized active returns: ratios of realized active returns to forecast active risk. Pooled over four months, the standard deviation of standardized active returns was 1.06, which according to χ^2 tests, was statistically consistent with the unbiased result of 1.0.

Finally using a variance-forecasting test suggested by Engle, Hong, and Kane (1990), we have run options-based tests comparing multiple-factor risk model forecasts with historical asset-by-asset risk. In these tests, we construct

30 random portfolios of 100, 150, 200, and 250 assets and generate the two forecasts of active risk. We then use the Black–Scholes model to price one-month at-the-money options on portfolio active value based on these two forecasts. We create a synthetic market in these options, trading at the mean price. At the end of the period, we calculate profit and loss. Over a 36-month period from January 1988 through December 1990, the strategy using the multiple-factor risk model forecasts, on average, returned 37 basis points per option traded with the historical volatility trader, with a standard deviation of 134 basis points. In this zero-sum game, the strategy based on historical volatility lost 37 basis points per option traded.

In both in-sample and out-of-sample tests of model validity, we occasionally invoke standard distributional assumptions to interpret the statistical significance of the results. Also, in both model building and testing, we make use of Monte Carlo simulations to test statistical significance while relaxing the required assumptions. As to investment significance, if some event occurs 3 times out of 12, an investor would want to know about it, even if a statistician would not be sure of its importance at the 95 percent confidence level.

Empirical observations concerning model validity are more vague than statistical tests, but they are still relevant. Simply put, these models successfully make use of intuitive factors to predict risk and understand return, and they have been widely accepted by the investment community for those roles for 18 years now.

How do multiple-factor risk models compare with their existing alternatives? Historical asset-by-asset covariance matrixes consistently underperform multiple-factor models in risk forecasting, and they suffer from severe estimation problems. A covariance matrix for 1,000 assets contains 500,500 independent entries, all estimated with errors. In addition, unless estimated over more than 1,000 time periods, the covariance matrix will not be full rank.

Simpler versions of the multiple-factor approach include a one-factor model and a constant-correlation model. The one-factor model is a close relative of the capital asset pricing model. This model includes only one common factor—the market. The constant-correlation model assumes that all assets exhibit the same correlation. Both models are simple and helpful for "quick and dirty" applications but ignore linkages among stocks in specific industries and with similar attributes.

Another approach to risk modeling uses statistical factor analysis. This approach identifies factors based on past correlations between asset returns. These factors are typically not intuitive or recognizable. This statistically driven approach can lead to risk forecasts comparable in quality to multiple-factor risk model forecasts but without any of the insight. Also, because they do not rely on investor intuition, they can be less robust than multiple-factor models.

Overall, multiple-factor risk models outperform all alternative risk models in providing incisive, intuitive, and interesting risk analysis.

Applications of Multiple-Factor Risk Models

The technical core of a multiple-factor risk model is the attribution of asset returns to chosen common factor and specific returns, plus forecasts of the variances and covariances of these common factor and specific returns. This technical core supports three separate types of investment analysis, which focus on the present, the future, and the past.

The Present: Current Portfolio Risk Analysis. The multiple-factor risk model decomposes current, overall portfolio risk in several ways. This decomposition of risk identifies the important sources of risk in the portfolio and links those sources with aspirations for active return.

One way to divide the risk is to identify the market and the residual components. An alternative is to look at risk relative to a benchmark and identify the active risk. A third way to divide the risk is between the model risk and the specific risk. The risk model can also perform marginal analysis, identifying which assets, at the margin, are most and least diversifying in the portfolio.

Risk analysis is important for both passive management and active management. Passive managers attempt to match their portfolio returns to a particular benchmark. They run index funds, but depending on the benchmark, the passive managers' portfolios may not include all the stocks in the benchmark. For example, a passive small-stock manager might face prohibitive transaction costs for holding the thousands of assets in a broad small-stock benchmark. Current portfolio risk analysis can tell a passive manager the active risk, or tracking error, of a portfolio relative to its benchmark. The tracking error is the volatility of the difference in return between the portfolio and the benchmark. Passive managers want minimum tracking error.

The goal of active managers is not to track the benchmark as closely as possible but to outperform the benchmark. Still, risk analysis is important in active management, to focus active strategies. Active managers want to take on risk only along those dimensions they believe they can outperform.

By suitably decomposing current portfolio risk, active managers can better understand the positioning of their portfolios. Risk analysis can tell them not only what their active risk is but also why and how to change it. Risk analysis can classify active bets into inherent bets, intentional bets, and incidental bets:

- *Inherent bets.* An active manager who is trying to outperform a benchmark (or the market) will have to bear the benchmark risk. This risk is a constant part of the task, not under the portfolio manager's control.

- *Intentional bets.* An active portfolio manager has identified stocks that he believes will do well and stocks that he believes will do poorly. The manager should expect that these stocks will appear as important marginal sources of active risk. This is welcome news: It tells the portfolio manager that he has taken active positions that are consistent with his beliefs.

- *Incidental bets.* These are unintentional side effects of a manager's active position. The manager has inadvertently created an active position on some factor that is a significant contributor to marginal active risk. For example, a manager who builds a portfolio by screening on yield will find a large incidental bet on industries that have higher than average yields. Are these industry bets intentional or incidental? Incidental bets often arise through incremental portfolio management, where a sequence of stock-by-stock decisions, each plausible in isolation, leads to accumulated incidental risk.

TABLE 1. Sample Portfolio

Stock	Shares	Weight
American Express	100	1.45%
AT&T	100	2.56
Chevron	100	4.26
Coca Cola	100	5.65
Walt Disney Productions	100	10.62
Dow Chemicals	100	3.84
DuPont	100	3.19
Eastman Kodak	100	3.08
Exxon	100	3.08
General Electric	100	5.43
General Motors	100	2.59
IBM	100	6.00
International Paper	100	5.10
Johnson & Johnson	100	6.99
McDonalds	100	2.80
Merck	100	10.89
Minnesota Mining and Manufacturing	100	6.29
Philip Morris	100	5.30
Procter & Gamble	100	7.02
Sears	100	3.00

To understand portfolio risk characterization more concretely, consider the following problem: Using as an investment portfolio the Major Market Index (MMI), a price-weighted index of 20 of the largest U.S. stocks, analyze its risk relative to the S&P 500 as of February 28, 1992. The portfolio's composition is given in Table 1.

Comparing risk factor exposures against the benchmark, this portfolio contains larger, less volatile stocks with higher leverage and foreign income and lower earnings variability—what one might expect from a large-stock portfolio versus a broader index. The portfolio also contains several industry bets.

The multiple-factor risk model forecasts 21.3 percent volatility for the portfolio and 20.8 percent volatility for the index. The portfolio tracking error is 4.7 percent. Assuming that active returns are normally distributed, the portfolio annual return will lie within 4.7 percent of the index annual return roughly two-thirds of the time. The model also can forecast the portfolio's beta—its exposure to movements of the index. Beta measures the portfolio's inherent risk. The MMI portfolio beta is 1.02. This implies that if the S&P 500 exceeded its expected return by 100 basis points, we would expect the portfolio return to exceed its expected return by 102 basis points.

The marginal contribution to tracking error—the increase in tracking error from a 1 percent increase in asset holding financed by a 1 percent decrease in cash—can be used to determine the most and least diversifying assets. A more detailed treatment of marginal contribution to tracking error is found in the mathematical appendix to this paper.

In this example, increasing the holdings in American Express would do most to reduce risk, and increasing holdings in Merck would do the most to concentrate the portfolio. These are also the lowest and highest weighted assets in the portfolio.

Looking Forward: Portfolio Construction. Given forecasts of expected returns, a multiple-factor risk model can help construct investment portfolios that optimally implement bets on those returns. The idea is to maximize utility, defined as risk-adjusted expected return:

$$U = \sum_{n=1}^{N} h_n r_n - \lambda \sum_{n,m=1}^{N} h_n V_{n,m} h_m. \tag{9}$$

Here, h_n is the holding of asset n, r_n is the expected return to asset n, and λ is a risk aversion parameter. The covariance, $V_{n,m}$, comes from the multiple-factor risk model. In typical examples, the holdings are active holdings relative to a benchmark and the expected returns are exceptional returns (alphas) relative to the benchmark. The quadratic optimization problem is solved to determine the optimal portfolio weights. Of course, in real life, the problem must account for transaction costs and add constraints and penalties.

Beyond providing risk forecasts, multiple-factor risk models can occasionally help with return forecasts. Although this is not the main focus of this type of model, the research needed to choose factors can identify those that generate exceptional return; value factors, for example, often generate exceptional return. Portfolios that implement such bets on factors are called *tilt funds*.

In portfolio construction, we assign forecasts of exceptional return to the stocks in the MMI portfolio and then optimally weight them to maximize risk-adjusted exceptional return relative to the S&P 500. In the portfolio shown in Table 2, we arbitrarily assigned 2 percent exceptional return forecasts to those stocks with ticker symbols that fell in the top half of the list alphabetically and -2 percent forecasts to the rest. The optimization procedure constructs a reweighted portfolio.

The alphas shown in Table 2 imply an initial portfolio alpha of -0.19 percent.

TABLE 2. Portfolio Construction Example

Stock	Alpha	Shares	Weight
American Express	2.0%	344	5.51%
AT&T	-2.0	237	6.76
Chevron	-2.0	0	0.00
Coca Cola	-2.0	69	3.95
Walt Disney Productions	2.0	108	11.46
Dow Chemicals	2.0	156	6.49
DuPont	2.0	275	9.16
Eastman Kodak	2.0	232	6.59
Exxon	2.0	313	11.99
General Electric	2.0	235	12.45
General Motors	2.0	160	4.10
IBM	2.0	113	6.60
International Paper	2.0	114	5.87
Johnson & Johnson	-2.0	24	1.64
McDonalds	-2.0	0	0.00
Merck	-2.0	27	2.78
Minnesota Mining and Manufacturing	-2.0	0	0.00
Philip Morris	-2.0	46	0.14
Procter & Gamble	-2.0	2	3.58
Sears	-2.0	66	1.11

With this reweighting, the tracking error moves slightly, from 4.68 percent to 4.71 percent, and the alpha of the portfolio moves to 1.21 percent. For reasons of risk control, the optimizer cannot eliminate the holdings of all the negative alpha stocks, but it does reduce those holdings and eliminates three of them from the portfolio.

The Past: Performance Analysis. Historical analysis of investment performance is important for understanding realized investment performance and for backtesting new investment strategies. Over any one period, the model can attribute returns to the factors and to specific asset returns. Then, linking many periods of attributed returns, it can analyze the series of returns to these various bets. This helps measure investment skill and value added.

Within the factor structure of the model, past returns can be attributed to bets on factors and bets on specific asset returns. For each historical period, we know the exposures of the portfolio relative to its benchmark, as well as the subsequent factor and specific returns. By examining many such periods, we can aggregate returns attributed to each factor and returns attributed to specific asset bets. With this time series of attributed returns, we can observe mean achieved returns. This time series, as well as the model itself, leads to estimates of the risk associated with those returns.

For example, we can compare the performance of the S&P 500 portfolio with the BARRA ALL-US Index, a broad index of more than 5,000 stocks, for the 65 months from September 30, 1986, through February 28, 1992. The S&P 500 outperformed the BARRA Index by 92 basis points a year, with an annualized risk of 2.78 percent. Decomposition of this risk and return by source shows that most of this active return arose from bets on the common factors:

	Annual Return	*Annual risk*
Active common factors	0.98%	2.66%
Specific asset selection	0.07	0.74
Market timing	−0.13	0.35

Given the large numbers of stocks in the portfolio, very little of the active return arose from specific asset selection. The market-timing component measures return contributions attributable to variation in portfolio beta over the time period. The beta of the S&P 500 versus the BARRA ALL-US was 0.97 in March 1992, but it does vary over time. The market-timing contribution of −13 basis points arises because that beta tended to be above its mean value in months when the BARRA Index excess return was below its mean value, and vice versa.

Among all the bets (policies) included in the S&P portfolio but in not the BARRA ALL-US benchmark, the best performing was a positive bet on foreign income, which gained 28 basis points a year; the worst performing was the size bet, which lost 29 basis points a year during this period.

Two particular statistics can help assess the skill and value added of the S&P portfolio. Letting R_{annual} represent annualized returns and M represent the number of observation periods, the t-statistic for the mean return is:

$$t = \frac{E(R_{annual})}{SD(R_{annual})} \, (\sqrt{M}). \tag{10}$$

This statistic measures whether the observed mean annualized return differs significantly from zero. It is one statistical measure of investment skill. If the t-statistic exceeds 2.0 and returns are normally distributed, then the probability that simple luck generated these returns is less than 5 percent.

Related to this distinction between skill and luck is the question of whether the manager has added investment value. The utility defined in equation (9) can be used to measure value added, or risk-adjusted active return. Detailed analysis shows that value added rises in proportion to the square of the manager's information ratio, IR, or the ratio of annual active return, α_{annual}, to annual active risk, ω_{annual}:

$$VA_{max} = \frac{1}{4\lambda}\left(\frac{\alpha_{annual}}{\omega_{annual}}\right)^2, \tag{11}$$

with

$$IR = \frac{\alpha_{annual}}{\omega_{annual}}. \tag{12}$$

Value added rises with the manager's information ratio, regardless of the level of risk aversion.

If the M periods of observation of these returns correspond to T years, then the information ratio is just the t-statistic divided by the square root of the number of years of observation:

$$IR = \frac{t\text{-stat}}{\sqrt{T}}. \tag{13}$$

Overall, the *t*-statistic measures the statistical significance of the return, but the information ratio also captures the risk–reward trade-off of the strategy and the manager's value added.[5] An information ratio of 0.5 observed over five years may be statistically more significant than an information ratio of 0.5 observed over one year, but the value added will be equal. The distinction between the *t*-statistic and the information ratio arises because the definition of value added is based on risk over a particular horizon, in this case one year.

Using the results of single-period performance attribution over M periods, this analysis of skill and value added can be applied factor by factor. This process will identify not only *whether* the manager has overall skill and has added value but also *where* the manager has skill and has added value. The result is a precise analysis of the manager's style. For the example above, the information ratios and *t*-statistics for each component of active return are as follows:

	Information Ratio	t-statistic
Active common factors	0.37	0.85
Specific asset selection	0.10	0.23
Market timing	−0.37	−0.86

Other Uses of Multiple-Factor Models. Portfolio managers are not the only users of multiple-factor risk models. Researchers, plan sponsors, and traders also find them helpful. Investment researchers use multiple-factor risk models to run controlled backtests of future investment strategies. For this, their needs are similar to those of portfolio managers. They need to implement strategies optimally on historical data and understand the subsequent performance of those strategies. Researchers can use backtests to enhance their strategies. They can also use performance analysis and portfolio risk characterization to improve their understanding of the bets they are testing.

Pension plan sponsors can use multiple-factor risk models to coordinate their multiple managers. Portfolio risk characterization allows them to understand any gaps or overlaps among their managers or in their asset allocation mixes. Plan sponsors also use performance analysis to assess their managers' value added and to check on their managers' styles.

Traders can use multiple-factor models in at least two ways. The models can aid in risk control during the course of trading. Multiple-factor models can also

[5] For a more detailed discussion of the information ratio and its relationship to skill and value added, see Grinold (1990).

aid in index arbitrage strategies through their use in constructing small baskets of stocks to track index futures optimally.

Conclusions

Multiple-factor risk models perform well in predicting investment risk and providing investment intuition. Across many asset classes and markets, these models identify incisive, intuitive, and important common factors affecting risk and return. They use intuitive, easy-to-understand factors to analyze investment risk and returns. They accurately forecast investment risk and help explain past returns, but they do not forecast returns.

Multiple-factor risk models can be used to analyze current portfolio risk, construct portfolios that optimally trade off risk with expected returns, and analyze skill and value added associated with past returns. They are an important tool for managing portfolios, conducting investment research, coordinating multiple managers, and trading.

Portfolio managers use multiple-factor risk models to (1) analyze their current risk and understand the size and location of their bets, (2) construct portfolios that optimally trade off risk against expected returns, and (3) analyze and provide insight into their past returns in order to understand their skill and value added. Researchers use multiple-factor risk models in similar ways to backtest and fine-tune strategies. Pension plan sponsors use multiple-factor risk models to coordinate their multiple managers and to understand gaps and overlaps in their asset allocation mixes. Traders use these models to control investment risk over short horizons.

Multiple-factor risk models are central to structured investing and are also extremely useful for traditional investment processes. Whether investors structure their portfolios within a strict risk–return framework or whether they simply pick stocks according to tradition, multiple-factor risk models help control and understand risk and also help understand past performance.

Appendix A

The risk model in matrix notation is written as

$$r = Xf + u,$$

where r is an N vector of a stock's excess returns, X is an N by K matrix of stock factor exposures, f is a K vector of factor returns, and u is an N vector of specific returns.

We assume:

- the specific returns, u, are uncorrelated with the factor returns, f; that is $\text{cov}\{u_n, f_k\} = 0$ for all n and k.
- the covariance of stock n's specific return, u_n, with stock m's specific return, u_m, is 0, if $m \neq n$; that is, $\text{cov}\{u_n, u_m\} = 0$ if $m \neq n$.

With these assumptions, we can express the N by N covariance matrix, V, of stock returns as:

$$V = XFX^T + \Delta,$$

where F is the K by K covariance matrix of the factor returns and Δ is the N by N diagonal matrix of specific variance.

A portfolio, P, is described by an N-element vector, h_p, that gives the portfolio's holdings in the N risky assets. The factor exposures of P are given by:

$$x_p = X^T h_p.$$

The variance of P is given by:

$$\sigma_p^2 = x_p^T F x_p + h_p^T \Delta h_p = h_p^T V h_p.$$

A similar formula lets us calculate active variance. If h_B is the benchmark holdings vector, then we can define:

$$h_A = h_p - h_B,$$

$$x_A = X^T h_A,$$

and

$$\sigma_A^2 = x_A^T F x_A + h_A^T \Delta h_A.$$

Notice that we have separated both total and active risk into common factor and specific components. This method works because factor risks and specific risks are uncorrelated.

We can also examine the marginal effects of any change in the portfolio. This type of sensitivity analysis allows us to see what factors and assets have the largest impact on risk. The marginal impact on risk is measured by the partial derivative of the risk with respect to the asset holding.

We can compute these marginal contributions for total risk and active risk. The N vector of marginal contributions to total risk is:

$$MCTR = \frac{V h_p}{\sigma_p}.$$

The $MCTR(n)$ is the partial derivative of σ_p with respect to $h_p(n)$. We can think of it as the change in portfolio risk given a 1 percent increase in the holding of asset n, which was financed by decreasing the cash account by 1 percent. The cash holding, $h_p(0)$, is given by:

$$h_p(0) = 1 - \sum_{n=1}^{N} h_p(n).$$

In a similar way, we can define the marginal contribution to active risk as:

$$MCAR = \frac{V h_A}{\sigma_A}.$$

Bibliography

Akaike, H. 1974(a). "Markovian Representation of Stochastic Processes and its Application to the Analysis of Autoregressive Moving Average Processes." *Annals of the Institute of Statistical Mathematics* 26:363–87.

———. 1974(b). "A New Look at the Statistical Identification Model." *IEEE Transactions on Automatic Control*, 716–23.

Berry, Michael A. 1988. "A Practical Perspective on Evaluating Mutual Fund Risk." *Investment Management Review* (March/April):78–86.

Berry, Michael A., Edwin Burmeister, and Marjorie B. McElroy. 1988. "Sorting Out Risks Using Known APT Factors." *Financial Analysts Journal* 44 (March/April):29–42.

Bollerslev, Tim, Ray Y. Chou, Narayanan Jayaraman, and Kenneth F. Kroner. 1992. "ARCH Modeling in Finance: A Selective Review of the Theory and Empirical Evidence, with Suggestions for Future Research." *Journal of Econometrics* 52 (April/May):5–59.

Brock, William A. 1982. "Asset Prices in a Production Economy." In *The Economics of Information and Uncertainty*, ed. J. McCall, 1–43. Chicago: The University of Chicago Press.

Brown, Stephen J. 1990. "Macroeconomic Factors and the Japanese Stock Market." In *Japanese Capital Markets*, eds. Edwin J. Elton and Martin J. Gruber, 175–92. New York: Harper and Row.

Brown, Stephen J., and Mark I. Weinstein. 1983. "A New Approach to Testing Asset Pricing Models: The Bilinear Paradigm." *Journal of Finance* 38 (June):711–43.

Burmeister, Edwin, and Marjorie B. McElroy. 1988. "Joint Estimation of Factor Sensitivities and Risk Premia for the Arbitrage Pricing Theory." *Journal of Finance* 43 (June):721–33.

Burmeister, Edwin, and Kent D. Wall. 1986. "The Arbitrage Pricing Theory and Macroeconomic Factor Measures." *The Financial Review* 21 (February):1–20.

Burmeister, Edwin, Kent D. Wall, and James D. Hamilton. 1986. "Estimation of Unobserved Expected Monthly Inflation Using Kalman Filtering." *Journal of Business and Economic Statistics* 4:147–60.

Chamberlain, G., and M. Rothschild. 1983. "Arbitrage, Factor Structure, and Mean–Variance Analysis on Large Asset Markets." *Econometrica* 51:1281–304.

Chen, Nai-fu. 1983. "Some Empirical Tests of the Theory of Arbitrage Pricing." *Journal of Finance* 38 (December):1392–414.

Chen, Nai-fu, and Jonathan E. Ingersoll, Jr. 1983. "Exact Pricing in Linear Factor Models with Finitely Many Assets: A Note." *Journal of Finance* 38 (June):985–88.

Chen, Nai-fu, Richard Roll, and Stephen A. Ross. 1986. "Economic Forces and the Stock Market." *Journal of Business* 59 (July):383–403.

Cho, D. Chinhyung. 1984. "On Testing the Arbitrage Pricing Theory: Inter-Battery Factor Analysis." *Journal of Finance 39* (December):1485–1502.

Cho, D. Chinhyung, Edwin Elton, and Martin Gruber. 1984. "On the Robustness of the Roll and Ross Arbitrage Pricing Theory." *Journal of Financial and Quanitative Analysis* 19 (March):1–10.

Cho, D. Chinhyung., C. S. Eun, and L. W. Senbet. 1986. "International Arbitrage Pricing Theory: An Empirical Investigation." *Journal of Finance* 41 (June):313–30.

Cho, D. Chinhyung, and William Taylor. 1987. "The Seasonal Stability of the Factor Structure of Stock Returns." *Journal of Finance* 42 (December):1195–211.

Connor, Gregory. 1984. "A Unified Beta Pricing Theory." *Journal of Economic Theory* 34:13–31.

Connor, Gregory, and Robert A. Korajczyk. 1986. "Performance Measurement with the Arbitrage Pricing Theory: A New Framework for Analysis." *Journal of Financial Economics* 15 (January/February):373–94.

———. 1988. "Risk and Return in an Equilibrium APT: Application of a New Test Methodology." *Journal of Financial Economics* 21 (September):255–89.

Copeland, Thomas E., and J. Fred Weston. 1988. *Financial Theory and Corporate Policy.* Reading, Mass.: Addison-Wesley Publishing Company.

Cox, John C., Jonathan E. Ingersoll, Jr., and Stephen A. Ross. 1985. "An Intertemporal General Equilibrium Model of Asset Prices." *Econometrica* 53:363–84.

Dhrymes, Phoebus, Irwin Friend, and Bulent Gultekin. 1984. "A Critical Reexamination of the Empiral Evidence on the Arbitrage Pricing Theory." *Journal of Finance* 39 (June):323–46.

Dybvig, Philip. 1983. "An Explicit Bound on Deviations from APT Pricing in a Finite Economy." *Journal of Financial Economics* 12 (December):483–96.

Dybvig, Philip H., and Stephen A. Ross. 1985. "Yes, the APT is Testable." *Journal of Finance* 40 (December):1173–88.

Elton, Edwin J., and Martin J. Gruber. 1970. "Homogeneous Groups and the Testing of Economic Hypotheses." *Journal of Financial and Quantitative Analysis* 5 (January):581–602.

———. 1971. "Improved Forecasting Through the Design of Homogenous Groups." *Journal of Business* 44 (October):432–50.

———. 1987. *Modern Portfolio Theory and Investment Analysis*, Third Edition. New York: John Wiley & Sons.

———. 1990. "A Multi-index Risk Model of the Japanese Stock Market." In *Japanese Capital Markets*, eds. Edwin J. Elton and Martin J. Gruber, 127–54. New York: Harper and Row.

Elton, Edwin J., Martin J. Gruber, and Prafulla Nabar. 1988. "Bond Returns, Immunization, and the Return Generating Process." *Studies in Banking and Finance* 5:125–54.

Engle, Robert F. 1982. "Autoregressive Conditional Heteroskedasticity with Estimates of the Variance of U.K. Inflation." *Econometrica* 51:987–1008.

Engle, Robert F, Che-Hsiung Hong, and Alex Kane. 1990. "Valuation of Variance Forecasts with Simulated Option Markets." *San Diego Economics Discussion Paper*, University of California.

Fama, Eugene F., and Kenneth R. French. 1992. "The Cross-Section of Expected Stock Returns." *Journal of Finance* 47 (June):427–65.

Fama, Eugene F., and James MacBeth. 1973. "Risk, Return, and Equilibrium: Empirical Tests." *Journal of Political Economy* (May/June):607–36.

Farrell, James. 1974. "Analyzing Covariation of Returns to Determine Homogeneous Stock Groupings." *Journal of Business 47* (April):186–207.

Francis, Jack Clark. 1991. *Investments: Analysis and Management*. New York: McGraw-Hill, Inc.

Gibbons, Michael R. 1982. "Multivariate Tests of Financial Models: A New Approach." *Journal of Financial Economics* 10 (March):3–27.

Grinold, Richard C. 1990. "The Fundamental Law of Active Management." In *Managing Institutional Assets*, ed. Frank J. Fabozzi. New York: Harper & Row.

Hamao, Yasushi. 1990. "An Empirical Examination of the Arbitrage Pricing Theory: Using Japanese Data." In *Japanese Capital Markets*, eds. Edwin J. Elton and Martin J. Gruber, 155–74. New York: Harper and Row.

Hansen, L. P., and S. F. Richard. 1987. "The Role of Conditioning Information in Deducing Testable Restrictions Implied by Dynamic Asset Pricing Models." *Econometrica* 55:587–613.

Huberman, Gur. 1982. "A Simple Approach to Arbitrage Pricing Theory." *Journal of Economic Theory* 78:183–91.

Huberman, Gur, and Robert Stambaugh. 1987. "Mimicking Portfolios and Exact Arbitrage Pricing." *Journal of Finance* 42 (March):1–9.

Ingersoll, Jonathan E. Jr. 1984. "Some Results in the Theory of Arbitrage Pricing." *Journal of Finance* 39 (September):1021–39.

Ingersoll, Jonathan E. Jr. 1987. *Theory of Financial Decision Making*. Totowa, NR: Rowman & Littlefield.

King, Benjamin F. 1966. "Market and Industry Factors in Stock Price Behavior." *Journal of Business* 39 (January):139–40.

Lawley, D. N., and A. E. Maxwell. 1971. *Factor Analysis as a Statistical Method*. New York: Macmillan.

Lehmann, Bruce N., and David M. Modest. 1987. "Mutual Fund Performance Evaluation: A Comparison of Benchmarks and Benchmark Comparisons." *Journal of Finance* 42 (June):233–65.

————. 1988. "The Empirical Foundations of the Arbitrage Pricing Theory." *Journal of Financial Economics* 20 (September):213–54.

Lintner, John. 1965a. "The Valuation of Risk Assets and the Selection of Risky Investments in Stock Portfolios and Capital Budgets." *Review of Economics and Statistics* (February):13–37.

————. 1965b. "Security Prices, Risk, and Maximal Gains from Diversification." *Journal of Finance* 20 (December):587–615.

Litzenberger, Robert H., and Krishna Ramaswamy. 1979. "The Effect of Personal Taxes and Dividends on Capital Asset Prices: Theory and Empirical Evidence." *Journal of Financial Economics* 72 (June):163–96.

Markowitz, Harry M. 1952. "Portfolio Selection," *Journal of Finance* 7 (March):77–91.

————. 1959. *Portfolio Selection: Efficient Diversification of Investments.* New York: John Wiley & Sons.

McElroy, Marjorie B., and Edwin Burmeister. 1988. "Arbitrage Pricing Theory as a Restricted Nonlinear Multiple Regression Model: ITNLSUR Estimates." *Journal of Business and Economic Statistics* 6:29–42.

McElroy, Marjorie B., Edwin Burmeister, and Kent D. Wall. 1985. "Two Estimators for the APT Model when Factors are Measured." *Economics Letters* 19:271–75.

Merton, Robert C. 1972. "An Analytical Derivation of the Efficient Portfolio." *Journal of Financial and Quantitative Analysis* 7 (September):1851–72.

Mossin, Jan. 1966. "Equilibrium in a Capital Asset Market." *Econometrica* (October):768–83.

Research Foundation of the Institute of Chartered Financial Analysts. 1991. *The Founders of Modern Finance: Their Prize Winning Concepts and 1990 Nobel Lectures.* Charlottesville, Va.

Roll, Richard, and Stephen A. Ross. 1980. "An Empirical Investigation of the Arbitrage Pricing Theory." *Journal of Finance* 35 (December):1073–103.

Rosenberg, Barr. 1974. "Extra-Market Components of Covariance in Security Returns—I." *Journal of Financial and Quantitative Analysis* 9 (March):263–74.

Rosenberg, Barr, and Vinay Marathe. 1975. "The Prediction of Investment Risk: Systematic and Residual Risk." *Proceedings of the Seminar on the Analysis of Security Prices,* University of Chicago (November):85–224.

————. 1979. "Test of Capital Asset Pricing Hypotheses." *Research in Finance* (annual):115–224.

Ross, Stephen A. 1976. "The Arbitrage Theory of Capital Asset Pricing." *Journal of Economic Theory* (December):341–60.

————. 1977. "Return, Risk, and Arbitrage." In *Risk and Return in Finance*, eds. I. Friend and J. Bicksler, 189–219. Cambridge, Mass.: Ballinger.

————. 1978. "Mutual Fund Separation in Financial Theory—The Separating Distribution." *Journal of Economic Theory* 17:254–86.

Ross, Stephen A., and Richard Roll. 1984. "The Arbitrage Pricing Theory Approach to Strategic Portfolio Planning." *Financial Analysts Journal* 40 (May/June):14–26.

Ross, Stephen A., and Randolph W. Westerfield. 1988. *Corporate Finance*. St. Louis: Times Mirror/Mosby College Publishing.

Rudd, Andrew, and Henry K. Clasing, Jr. 1988. *Modern Portfolio Theory*, Second Edition, Orinda, California: Andrew Rudd.

Schwartz, G. 1978. "Estimating the Dimension of a Model." *Annals of Statistics* 6:461–64.

Sharpe, William F. 1964. "Capital Asset Prices: A Theory of Market Equilibrium Under Conditions of Risk." *Journal of Finance* 19 (September):425–42.

————. 1977. "The Capital Asset Pricing Model: A 'Multi-Beta' Interpretation." In *Financial Decision Making Under Uncertainty*, eds. Haim Levy and Marshall Sarnat. New York: Academic Press.

————. 1984. "Factor Models, CAPMs, and the APT." *Journal of Portfolio Management* 11 (Fall):21–25.

Treynor, Jack L. 1961. "Toward a Theory of the Market Value of Risky Assets." Unpublished manuscript.

Trzcinka, C. 1986. "On the Number of Factors in the Arbitrage Pricing Model." *Journal of Finance* 41 (June):347–68.

Wei, K. C. John. 1988. "An Asset-Pricing Theory Unifying the CAPM and APT." *Journal of Finance* 43 (September):881–92.

Selected AIMR Publications*

Quality Management and Institutional Investing, 1994 . . . . $20
   Keith P. Ambachtsheer, *Editor*

Managing Emerging Market Portfolios, 1994 . . . . $20
   John W. Peavy III, CFA, *Editor*

Global Asset Management and Performance Attribution, 1994 . . . . $20
   Denis S. Karnosky, Ph.D., and Brian D. Singer, CFA

Franchise Value and the Price/Earnings Ratio, 1994 . . . . $20
   Martin L. Leibowitz and Stanley Kogelman

Investing Worldwide, 1993, 1992, 1991, 1990 . . . . $20 each

Derivative Strategies for Managing Portfiolio Risk, 1994 . . . . $20
   Keith C. Brown, CFA, *Editor*

The Modern Role of Bond Covenants, 1994 . . . . $20
   Ileen B. Malitz

Equity Securities Analysis and Evaluation, 1994 . . . . $20

**The CAPM Controversy: Policy and Strategy Implications
for Investment Management**, 1993 . . . . $20
   Diana R. Harrington and Robert A. Korajczyk, *Editors*

The Health Care Industry $20
   James Balog, *Editor*

**Predictable Time-Varying Components of International
Asset Returns**, 1993 . . . . $20
   Bruno Solnik

The Oil and Gas Industries, 1993 . . . . $20
   Thomas A. Petrie, CFA, *Editor*

**Execution Techniques, True Trading Costs, and the
Microstructure of Markets**, 1993 . . . . $20
   Katrina F. Sherrerd, CFA, *Editor*

Investment Counsel for Private Clients, 1993 . . . . $20
   John W. Peavy III, CFA, *Editor*

Active Currency Management, 1993 . . . . $20
   Murali Ramaswami

The Retail Industry, 1993 . . . . $20
   Charles A. Ingene, *Editor*

Equity Trading Costs, 1993 . . . . $20
   Hans R. Stoll

Options and Futures: A Tutorial, 1992 . . . . $20
   Roger G. Clarke

*A full catalog of publications is available from AIMR, P.O. Box 7947, Charlottesville, Va. 22906 U.S.A.;
804/980-3647; fax 804/977-0350.

Order Form

Additional copies of *A Practitioner's Guide to Factor Models* (and other publications listed on page 86) are available for purchase. The price is **$20 each in U.S. dollars**. Simply complete this form and return it via mail or fax to:

AIMR
Publications Sales Department
P.O. Box 7947
Charlottesville, Va. 22906
U.S.A.
Telephone: 804/980-3647
Fax: 804/977-0350

Name _____

Company _____

Address _____

_____ Suite/Floor _____

City _____

State _____ ZIP _____ Country _____

Daytime Telephone _____

Title of Publication	**Price**	**Qty.**	**Total**

Shipping/Handling
- ☐ All U.S. orders: Included in price of book
- ☐ Air mail, Canada and Mexico: $5 per book
- ☐ Surface mail, Canada and Mexico: $3 per book
- ☐ Air mail, all other countries: $8 per book
- ☐ Surface mail, all other countries: $6 per book

Discounts
- ☐ Students, professors, university libraries: 25%
- ☐ CFA candidates (ID #_____): 25%
- ☐ Retired members (ID #_____): 25%
- ☐ Volume orders (50+ books of same title): 40%

Discount $__−_____

4.5% sales tax (Virginia residents) $_____

8.25% sales tax (New York residents) $_____

7% GST (Canada residents) $_____

Shipping/handling $_____

Total cost of order $_____

☐ Check or money order enclosed payable to **AIMR**   ☐ Bill me

Charge to: ☐ VISA   ☐ MASTERCARD   ☐ AMERICAN EXPRESS

Card Number: _____ ☐ Corporate ☐ Personal

Signature: _____ Expiration date: _____